# Liberals for Lunch

# LIBERALS FOR LUNCH

## Cal Thomas

## Cartoons by Wayne Stayskal

CROSSWAY BOOKS • WESTCHESTER, ILLINOIS
A Division of Good News Publishers

Cover designed by K. L. Mulder
Illustrations by Wayne Stayskal

First printing, 1985.

Printed in the United States of America.

Library of Congress Catalog Card Number 85-71100

ISBN 0-89107-366-3

# Dedication page

To the memory of my father, Clinton Samuel Thomas, and to my mother, Barbara Elizabeth Thomas. From you I received more than my looks, hair, color, and height. I also received the love and encouragement I needed to believe that I could accomplish anything, if I would only try.

And to my brother, Marshall, who, because he is mentally retarded, will never know the success I have enjoyed, but for whom perfection waits ahead when God shall wipe away every tear and restore the years the locusts have eaten.

# Acknowledgments

The author wishes to thank a number of people, without whose help, encouragement, and approval he would not now be writing for the Los Angeles Times Syndicate.

First, special thanks to Tom Johnson, publisher of the *Los Angeles Times,* who believed enough in me to give me a chance to share my perspectives with newspaper readers around the country.

Second, Richard Newcombe and Kathy Newton. Thank you for buying my lunch that March day in 1984 (and also buying my column!). Your encouragement has meant a lot to me. Thanks, too, to Willard Colston, chairman of the Syndicate, who gave the final approval for the column.

Third, my daily thanks to Dan Pollack and Connie Kloos, the two copy editors who, after handling the likes of Art Buchwald, Joseph Kraft, Henry Kissinger, and Erma Bombeck, still have time for somebody like me. In television, an editor can make or break a correspondent. In newspaper writing, a good editor is the key to success. Dan and Connie, you are two of the best, and I genuinely love and admire you both.

Fourth, a special thanks to Bob Berger, who decides what goes in and what doesn't go in the *Los Angeles Times* Opinion Page. The *L.A. Times* has over one million readers a day, and for someone like Bob Berger to believe that what you have to say deserves to be read makes you believe in miracles!

Lastly, and most important of all, I want to give glory and honor to God who has allowed me to have this privilege and without Whose intervention none of this would have been possible.

# Contents

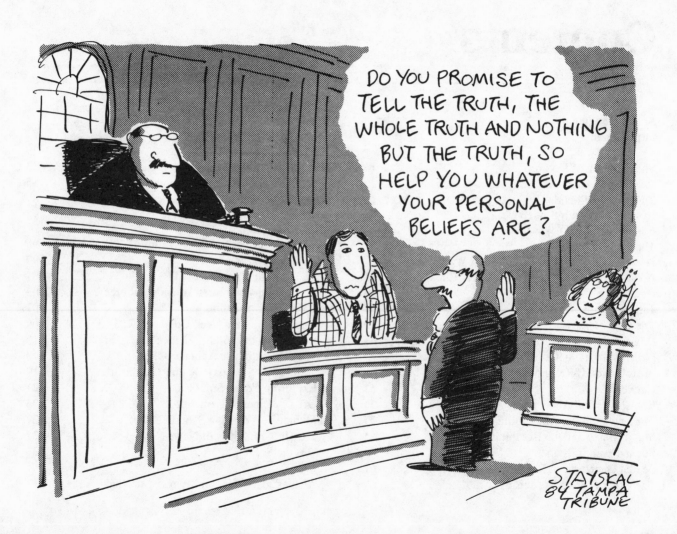

# Introduction

Everywhere one looks there is criticism of the media, by which I mean television, newspapers, movies, and magazines, but primarily television and newspapers. Surveys have shown that we rely more on television for our news and information than on any other source. Newspapers tend to exert more long-term influence on decision-makers, particularly those in government. Curiously, while relying on television and newspapers, we also have far less confidence that what we are receiving is fair and accurate. It is what I would call a "Listerine complex." We hate them, but we view or read them at least twice a day!

Much of the criticism of the media, particularly journalism, is by now familiar. George Keyworth, who heads the White House Office of Science and Technology, spoke for many of the critics when he charged that the American press, "drawn from a narrow fringe element on the far left of our society," is trying to tear down America and has done an irresponsible job of reporting.

Keyworth said the press is out of step with trends in America and "skewed toward an apparent joy in attacking anything that resembles the 'establishment.'"

Author and commentator Benjamin J. Stein wrote a column for *The Wall Street Journal* in which he described television as a "religious wasteland." Said Stein, "With the exception of an occasional attempt to put sex into the convent, such as 'Shattered Vows,' religion and the appeal to religious values in decision-making are simply invisible in prime-time television today . . . prime-time network television became an island without religion in an ever-more religious America. It has something to do with the people who make television, something to do with network skittishness, and something to do with politics."

The same could be said of newspapers. Yes, there is a "religion page," just as there is an obituary page (the two are not necessarily unrelated in the eyes of some editors). But the only kind of religion or religious values that make the front page or the editorial pages have been, until recently, a scandal or the Pope's latest pronouncement on birth control or abortion, a pronouncement that is guaranteed to bring criticism and derision.

Books have been written on press bias. It is easy to analyze and to diagnose. What is difficult is to do something that will bring about change.

Until recently, most who wear the label "conservative" or "Christian" (the two are not necessarily synonymous in all cases), have contented themselves with criticism of the "left-wing" press. Now there are movements afoot to do what should have been done a long time ago. The First Amendment grants freedom to the press. It does not guarantee the right of the current crowd to own and control it in perpetuity.

The press is a business before it is anything else. If conservatives would begin buying up media outlets with the goal, not of doing unto the left what the left has done unto the right, but of establishing true fairness and balance in news and entertainment programming, we would then begin to see just whose ideas are better.

We must also begin to affirm young people who possess the necessary gifts to participate in the media. For too long our churches have affirmed only those who wish to enter what we unbiblically refer to as "full-time Christian service" (is there such a thing as "half-time Christian service?). Students need to know that if they have been equipped by God with talents for journalism that can be enhanced by study and practical experience, their church and peer group will stand behind them with as much support as they do the person who is going to another mission field in Africa. Notice I said "another" mission field. Journalism, the arts, law, medicine, whatever, are also mission fields that have gone sour because of our placing them outside the "approved" sphere for Christians.

Another avenue that has been all but avoided is the placing of our ideas on the editorial pages of the nation's newspapers. Until recently this has been nearly impossible (William F. Buckley, Jr. and, more recently, George F. Will and Patrick J. Buchanan, new director of White House Communications, have been the exceptions).

In the Fall of 1983, I wrote a column based on my book, *Book Burning,* which is a book about censorship. I sent the column to the *New York Times,* the least likely paper in the country to print it. The editor called me and in a burst of tokenism printed the column (I haven't been in the *Times* since!). I began to write other columns. They were carried by *The Washington Post, Los Angeles Times,* and *USA Today.*

I contacted syndicates which distribute the best-known columnists to newspapers throughout the country. The replies were friendly and complimentary ("you write well, but . . ."). There were no takers.

I remembered that Tom Johnson, who worked in the Lyndon Johnson (no relation) administration while I was with NBC News, was now publisher of the *Los Angeles Times.* I called him and said I thought there was a lack of good conservative commentary in the nation's newspapers. He agreed. This was shortly after a *Time* magazine cover story on the lack of trust held by many Americans in the press.

Tom said that the next time I came to Los Angeles he would arrange for me to have lunch with the people who run the Los Angeles Times Syndicate.

In March 1984, I flew to Los Angeles and had lunch with Richard Newcombe, vice president of the Syndicate, and Cathy Newton, the chief copy editor (both have since left for other positions).

To my utter astonishment, they asked if I could write two columns per week, beginning April 17.

As a Christian, there is no doubt in my mind that God has allowed me this marvelous opportunity so that something of "the mind of Christ" can be considered on the editorial pages of our nation's newspapers. Not every column is overtly "religious." In fact, most are not. But if you read carefully between the lines (and if you read carefully between the lines of people who do not share my world view, you will see their prejudices and beliefs revealed as well), you will be able to detect Who and what gives me my perspective.

My good friend Wayne Stayskal has been doing this for years. Wayne is one of the most accomplished political cartoonists in the country. You see his cartoons on editorial pages all over America. He draws now for the *Tampa Tribune* and is syndicated through the Chicago Tribune Syndicate.

As in my columns, you can see in Wayne's pithy and often hilarious drawings something of "the mind of Christ" and a Biblical world view. He is not "preachy," but he makes his points with wit and skill. I am personally honored and delighted that Wayne has agreed to provide some of his excellent drawings to complement my columns in this book.

History is a battle of ideas, but if we who are Christians and/or conservatives do not have our ideas before the people on the same battlefield on which the war is being fought, what good are we? What impact can we possibly expect to have if we remain content with writing, speaking, and otherwise communicating only with each other?

The purpose of this book is not just to inform and entertain. If you live in an area that carries my column (at this writing, about thirty towns and cities), I hope that you will read them in your local paper and write letters to the editor in support of me. That goes for Wayne Stayskal's cartoons as well.

What we have lacked, particularly in the Christian community, is a spirit of "oneness" and family that supports one another as we seek to exercise our various gifts in a way that will honor Jesus Christ.

You may agree or disagree from time to time with what we have to say, but we are trying to share our thoughts with people who need to hear another perspective than the one they are used to.

We ask no favors. We only want to be judged on our journalistic skills and merits. We believe we are saying (and drawing) something that is of interest to millions of Americans.

"I LOVE YOU, CINDY... WILL YOU MARRY ME FOR A YEAR OR TWO?

# The children of divorce

I saw a statistic the other day.
She could not have been more than eight or nine. She sat across the aisle from me on an airplane, clutching a new Cabbage Patch doll.

The little girl was dressed nicely enough, but she was crying. There were no audible sobs. Only tears which had produced red, puffy eyes. This was no recent injury that might have come from a lost puppy or stolen bicycle. This was a toothache kind of hurt—relentless and difficult to suppress.

I resisted the urge to move to the empty seat next to the little girl for fear she might have been forewarned not to speak to strangers and so I asked the flight attendant whether there was anything she might do to comfort the little girl.

The flight attendant whispered so as not to be overheard, "Oh, we get these kinds all the time."

"These kinds?" I said. "What do you mean, 'these kinds'?"

"The children of divorce," she said, "being shuttled back and forth between parents."

The flight attendant sat down beside the little girl and tried to comfort her. It was my turn to cry.

The children of divorce. Almost nightly we are exposed on television news to the faces of the children of war, but how many consider the pain suffered by the children of divorce?

Ironically, I had just finished reading an article in the airline magazine which said that about half of all marriages in America end in divorce and that infidelities occur in one-third of the marriages which last more than ten years.

These are statistics, but the statistic I saw across the aisle was flesh and blood; a child longing to be held and loved unconditionally by both parents at the same time, under the same roof.

It is peculiar how one can speak dispassionately of the statistics of divorce and infidelity. It is almost clinical. But when one sees statistics as they really are, perspectives change.

I am not a psychologist or a sociologist, but could one reason why marriages fail and infidelities abound and so many little girls (and little boys) get hurt and cry be the result of a commitment phobia? Everything in our culture is made to become obsolete, including relationships. Everything is disposable. "Tear down paradise, put up a parking lot.'' Disposable bottles and cans. Disposable babies. Disposable marriages.

But what about the consequences, the hurt, the pain—psychological, emotional and physical—of those who have bought the lie and accepted the worship of the god Eros as the ultimate idolatry?

In *The Four Loves,* C. S. Lewis writes, "The grim joke is that this Eros whose voice seems to speak from the eternal realm is not himself necessarily even permanent . . . The world rings with complaints of his fickleness. What is baffling is the combination of this fickleness with his protestations of permanency. To be in love is both to intend and to promise lifelong fidelity. Love makes vows unasked; can't be deterred from making them . . .''

The temple of Eros has become our established church. It is in Eros, not God, that we trust.

Are we really better off after we jettison our first, second, or third wife (or husband) and kids? What are we searching for and is it worth the rubble we leave behind . . . the rubble of broken lives and tearful little girls?

I wish that Thomas Jefferson had not written about "the pursuit of happiness" as an "inalienable right." Properly understood, happiness is a byproduct of something else. It cannot be obtained by pursuing, anymore than the beauty of summer clouds can be grasped and placed in a bottle for future enjoyment.

Will the executive suite be enough to replace the hugs and kisses of a little girl who wants to feel loved and accepted in a stable home environment? Will the scars from broken relationships be healed by establishing new relationships without commitment? Happiness comes from commitment to spouse and children " 'til death do us part.''

Why do we never read in *Cosmo* or *Playboy* about the men and women who have gone bankrupt from buying into the "do your own thing" lifestyle? We only read of those who have taken off on their flights of fancy to Fantasy Island, never of those who have crash-landed.

What do we really have when we "have it all" if we leave crying little girls in our wake? Can we really say we are a success when we earn six-figure incomes and are sequestered in private offices, but have left the debris of failed marriages and psychologically damaged children behind? What shall it profit a man (or woman) if he gains the whole world and loses his own children?

As a reporter for twenty-one years, I have known five Presidents, traveled throughout much of the world, had the heady experience of being asked for my autograph, and enjoyed the praise of a small number of people. None of that has meant as much as the hugs and kisses I have received from my children (and wife!) and the voluntary acknowledgments of their love for me.

You can't hang that on the wall to impress colleagues, but you can hide it in your heart to comfort you in your old age.

# Bombs and abortion

The bombings at an abortion clinic and a family planning center in the Maryland suburbs of Washington have been instructive in one respect. We now know what upsets prochoicers. It is not the unrestricted destruction of human life inside the buildings where abortion is performed that angers them; rather, it is the destruction of the buildings.

Since 1973 when the Supreme Court legalized abortion-on-demand, more than fifteen million unborn lives have been snuffed out at 2908 abortion clinics.

Since 1982 there have been three hundred bombings on property where abortions are performed. Virtually all have occurred when the clinics were closed, so there have been no deaths or injuries reported.

The outrage expressed by the prochoicers over the bombings is hypocritical in the extreme. One would think they are referring to the abortion "doctors" instead of to the antiabortion bombers.

The *New York Times* described the bombings as a new form of domestic terrorism. It said the incidents were the products of warped minds and that decency requires that such actions be denounced.

National Organization for Women President Judy Goldsmith, who has not been heard from since the "gender gap" myth exploded on Election Day, blamed President Reagan for the bombings. Goldsmith said the President is at fault because he is opposed to abortion and has compared it to the Holocaust and called it murder.

Could Goldsmith and her feminist colleagues be charged with encouraging women to have abortions by referring to "products of conception" instead of "babies"?

The line I liked best came from Jayne Bray, a member of the Pro-Life Nonviolent Action Committee. Echoing the meaningless campaign rhetoric of Geraldine Ferraro and New York Gov. Mario Cuomo, Bray put her tongue in her cheek and said, "I am personally opposed to the destruction of property, but I respect the right of people who do it where babies are being slaughtered."

Tactically, as well as politically, the bombing of abortion clinics is probably not a good idea. It allows the prochoicers to shift the debate from what is taking place inside the buildings to what is taking place outside.

Prolife groups, however, continue to be denied access to the media with their most compelling argu-

"NO, NO, WORLEY. WHEN I SAID GUARD THE ABORTION CLINIC SO NOBODY WOULD GET KILLED, I MEANT ARREST BOMBERS, NOT ABORTIONISTS!"

ment against abortion. That argument is rooted in pictures of the unborn and of what actually takes place during an abortion. Once the word (or in this case, the picture) is out, the argument between "product of conception" and "baby" will quickly be brought to an end.

Until then, we are likely to see more of these bombing incidents, just as we did during the 1960s when blacks, frustrated by peaceful attempts to win their civil rights, decided to take matters into their own hands and direct the attention of the country to their plight.

A national debate on abortion is long overdue. It is only when that debate is allowed to take place that we can expect the bombings to stop.

"IF WE EVER DECIDE TO GIVE THE AMERICANS ON-SITE INSPECTION OF THESE MISSILES THE SITES WILL BE WASHINGTON, NEW YORK, CHICAGO, LOS ANGELES ... "

# Logic turned inside out

At least eleven self-styled "Christian antiwar groups" have developed a contingency plan to protest a U.S. invasion of Nicaragua. The plan is the child of the Sojourners Community, a group of "aging young people" who think the Vietnam war is still going on.

Resplendent in beards, beads, and bib overalls, these prisoners of a 1970 time capsule plan to take over the field office of each U.S. senator and representative until the member votes to end the invasion. Their contingency plan also calls for them to engage in "nonviolent civil disobedience at the White House to demand an end to the invasion." That is more than the opponents of the ruling Ortega brothers can do in Managua.

On a scale of 1 to 10, I would say that the chance of a U.S. invasion of Nicaragua is about a 2, but the chance of a Cuban-backed Sandinista invasion of Honduras, Guatemala, or Costa Rica is a 12. Instead of contingency planning for a U.S. invasion in Central America, these so-called antiwar groups ought to develop contingency plans in the event that Castro is successful and all of Central America becomes his fiefdom.

The certain disaster would include a tidal wave of "feet people" to our poorly policed borders. Already, according to the U.S. Embassy in San Salvador, one out of nine Salvadorans is in the United States. That adds up to 500,000 people. It takes no imagination to foresee what would happen if El Salvador with five million, Panama with two million, Honduras with 3.8 million, Guatemala with 7.2 million, or Mexico with seventy-six million fell to Fidel.

Richard Holwill, a deputy assistant secretary of state for international affairs, has a question for the Sojourners crowd. He wants to know how peacefully these "antiwar groups" will sleep at night if the Sandinista airfields are turned into bases for nuclear missiles, Backfire bombers and a center for guerrilla war, drug exportation, and terrorism. Mr. Holwill says the goal of the Reagan administration is to deny the Soviet Union a base for unconventional warfare of this type. He says what the Sojourners people forget is that the world is more peaceful when you do not let others threaten you.

Virginia Polk, a policy analyst at the Heritage Foundation in Washington, says there will be other consequences from a collapse in Central America. She says an enormous defense effort will be required, necessitating the recall of forces from Europe, reinstitution of the draft, higher taxes to pay for it all, and more men under arms than ever before. Considering these prospects, the line, "We can fight them in El Salvador or in El Paso," does not seem as glib as it once sounded.

Who are some of these "peace groups"? One is the Fellowship of Reconciliation. According to *Information Digest,* one of FOR's staff members, Dan Ebner, has written, "As a Catholic, a pacifist, a feminist and a Socialist, I am committed to working for the anti-imperialist, antiracist, antisexist, and anti-interventionist movement." Geraldine Ferraro, meet a guy who doesn't think his faith should be a "private matter."

Another group in the contingency planning is Clergy and Laity Concerned, which described its goals in January 1970 this way: "What we are about today is not simply an end to the war in Vietnam, but a struggle against American imperialism and exploitation in just about every corner of the world. . . . Our task is to join those who are angry and who hate the corporate power which the United States presently represents, and to attempt, in our struggle, to liberate not only black, brown, and yellow men in every corner of the world, but more importantly, to help liberate our own nation from its reactionary and exploitative policies." The Soviets could not have put it better.

These so-called "antiwar groups" are again suffering from a case of logic turned inside out. They told us there would not be a bloodbath in Vietnam when the United States pulled out, and now they tell us that the only way to peace in Nicaragua and in all of Central America is for us to stay out. Some of the "antiwar groups" said the same thing about Europe in the 1930s, remember?

Neville Chamberlain, we who are about to die salute you!

# How to deal with Soviets? Ask the man who was one

Back in the days before "recall" became a part of the automobile vocabulary, the Packard Motor Co. had a slogan, "Ask the man who owns one." Packard felt that its satisfied customers were the company's best promoters for convincing potential buyers of the car's merits.

I thought of that slogan while pondering the soon-to-be resumed (if you are on the American side) or new (if on the Soviet side) arms control negotiations. Of all the experts one could ask for advice on how best to deal with the Soviets, why not ask the man who was one?

In this case, the man is Arkady Shevchenko, the highest-ranked Soviet official ever to defect to the West. When he defected in 1978, Mr. Shevchenko was Soviet ambassador to the United Nations in charge of the National Security Council and Political Affairs.

*Southern Partisan Magazine* interviewed Mr. Shevchenko (Winter 1984), and his views stand in sharp contrast to those Americans who are calling for "flexibility," "compromise," and "concessions" by the U.S. side even before the bargaining begins.

Mr. Shevchenko's advice for avoiding nuclear war? "Be extremely strong. That is what they understand …presently, their global strategy is to reach their objectives without nuclear war."

Are the Soviets close to launching a nuclear attack against the United States? Not according to Mr. Shevchenko: "They are not going to launch an attack under the present circumstances for a while. But if the United States becomes weaker and weaker and weaker, then I cannot say what will happen in ten or fifteen years."

What about the advisability of engaging the Soviets in talks? A good idea, says Mr. Shevchenko, but he advises the U.S. side to keep one hand on its wallet:

"Whatever they agree to, if they agree to control or freeze weapons, they will be lying, trying to deceive the whole world in agreeing to a freeze. What they agree to will have no control over what they do."

Mr. Shevchenko has high praise for the way President Reagan has been handling the Soviets. He gives him good marks for his strong language outlining the U.S. position and the U.S. view of the Soviet position.

He supports the Grenada operation as a needed catharsis which spoke louder than words.

He advises that in talks with the Soviets, the United States should not let them set the agenda, but insist on talking about a full range of issues, including Poland and Afghanistan.

Mr. Shevchenko, of course, is not the only one chiding the United States about its often self-deluded view of the Soviet system.

Alexander Solzhenitsyn has been saying it and writing it for years. More recently, so have Victor Herman, an American who was trapped in the Soviet purge vacuum of the 1930s, spending most of his youth in prison for nothing at all, and Jan Sejna, a top Czech official who defected to the West in 1968.

Mr. Sejna told the London *Sunday Telegraph* that the Kremlin is no more interested in real détente today than it was in the 1960s. Said he, "The Russians see détente as nothing more than a strategy of deception. They never change their strategy, only their tactics to suit the moment."

Does anyone at the White House or State Department need a real "expert" to take along to Geneva in January? Mr. Shevchenko, Mr. Solzhenitsyn, Mr. Herman, or Mr. Sejna might be available. They know the Soviet mindset, and you can't get much better advice than from those who were once part of the system.

Worse advice than none at all is good advice that is not heeded. Is anybody listening?

# The nuns get the word

The Vatican's threat of retaliation against twenty-four American nuns who signed a "pro-choice" newspaper ad is the latest attempt by Pope John Paul II to put a halt to the rampant liberalism within the Roman Catholic Church. At issue is who speaks for the church and what is the role of priests, nuns, and bishops when the Vatican expounds on doctrinal issues.

The ad, published during the presidential campaign, suggested that there is no authentic Catholic position on abortion. Archbishop John J. O'Connor of New York strongly disagreed and publicly took on two of the country's best-known Catholic politicians, New York Gov. Mario Cuomo and Democratic vice presidential candidate Geraldine Ferraro, both of whom had made their "prochoice" positions clear.

The reason for the confusion (and for the pope's decision to tighten the reins on everything from liberation theology, to priests serving in government, to the autonomy of Catholics deciding for themselves what is to be taught as Catholic doctrine) can be blamed on a misunderstanding of the collegiality which the Second Vatican Council encouraged.

During this almost laissez-faire period, many Catholic theoreticians, scholars, bishops, priests, and nuns decided to "do their own thing." The result was creeping modernism and an accommodation with the spirit of the age.

In his latest pronouncement on official church teachings, "Reconciliation and Penance," the pope has taken a "back-to-basics" approach. Beginning with the subjects of sin and repentance, the pope goes on to chastise those who dissent from Catholic theology, calling them contrary to the faith. While not retreating from his commitment to social justice, the pope again objects to the substitution of Marx, or any other philosophy, for Christ.

The central question in all of these debates within the church hierarchy over the past two decades, apart from the immediate subject of contention, has been, who is to decide the nature of truth so far as Catholic doctrine is concerned? This has nothing to do with the many gray areas that exist in all faiths, but of certain basic tenets that make a Catholic a Catholic, and without which a person cannot be called a Catholic, no matter what else he or she may do.

Father Richard R. Roach, S.J., associate professor of moral theology at Marquette University in Milwaukee, believes that some Catholics lost their faith during this period of mushrooming liberalism, but, like defeated politicians who can't seem to tear themselves away from Washington, these liberal churchpersons did not want to leave the church.

Father Roach says the error of those who signed the "prochoice" abortion statement is the same as that committed by liberation theologists and their fellow travelers; namely, belief that the church is a political party which is susceptible to lobbying. They see themselves, he says, as a kind of "platform committee" that is trying to get its planks included in an overall policy statement which is constantly in flux. They do not believe that the church, Scripture, tradition, or the consistent teaching of popes past and present should be the arbiters of truth. To Pilate's question, "What is truth?" these religious lone rangers would reply, "Let's take a vote."

Father Roach says the dissenting nuns, priests, and lay people who signed the ad, publicly disagreeing with official teaching, are confusing the flock by suggesting that truth and doctrine can be determined by majority rule or a polling of the membership. It is for this reason, he says, that the pope is tightening his control over the church's liberal wing and refusing to allow it to go unchallenged when it publicly questions the authority of Rome.

It is not a question of whether the twenty-four nuns and the others who signed the ad are to be denied freedom of speech, as some have suggested. It is a question of who speaks for the Catholic Church. If the signers wish to have total freedom of speech, they should not have placed themselves under the authority of the church in the first place.

It has been said that the time to criticize the military is before joining the service. One presumably knows what is required when one takes the oath on induction day. The same can be said of those who take upon themselves the offices and responsibilities of bishops, priests, and nuns.

To allow anyone to determine authentic church teaching is to sow the seeds for ultimate chaos and falsehood which will lead many astray and turn the church into an agent of darkness rather than a lamp of light.

# Prodigal children have lost their way

In the parable of the prodigal son, we are told that the young man, after spending his inheritance on "wine, women and song," at last "came to his senses."

For the past twenty years, the USA has been on a narcissistic binge. One of the consequences has been a 300 percent rise in teenage suicides, from roughly six per 100,000 in 1964 to more than twenty-one today. An estimated 7,000 teenagers commit suicide each year. Another 400,000 try but fail. Why?

I believe it is because of unfulfilled expectations. From Hollywood films to television, popular music and magazines, teenagers are encouraged to become adults long before they are ready.

Sexual license is as sought after today as a driver's license. If a car is wrecked, a driver's license may be revoked. The culture refuses to revoke sexual license, no matter how many wrecks occur. Having received no hope from the culture, many young people divorce themselves from it by taking their lives.

There may never have been a greater assault on the moral reservoir of any nation since the pagan rituals of the Roman Empire. Those who take offense at criticism of films or magazines or music in the name of the First Amendment need to understand that the "freedom of choice" they advocate should be based on freedom of access to information.

Teenagers exposed to a monolithic view of life are programmed to accept that view. They are given no alternatives to sex, to drugs, to suicide. They ask, "Is that all there is?" The question echoes in a cavern of moral relativism.

Like the prodigal son, we need to come to our senses and realize that we have contributed to the moral cancers now eating away at our country.

Nearly twenty years ago, folk singer Pete Seeger wrote a protest song against the Vietnam war and President Johnson. One line said, "We're knee-deep in the big muddy and the big fool says to push on."

Today we are knee-deep in another "big muddy" and the "big fools" who tell our kids to do whatever they wish, that there are no absolute moral values, want us to push on, despite conclusive proof that their philosophy has failed.

The remedy for America's skyrocketing teenage suicide rate lies in a return to traditional values—family integrity, religious commitment, political involvement—which became traditional in the first place because they worked.

Teenagers alone are not responsible. It is a failure of adult commitment to one another in marriage and of commitment to children as something more than a tax deduction.

The need for a change is evident. Like the warning label on cigarettes, however, the warning signs of cultural decadence can help us only if we "come to our senses."

"I WENT OVER OUR FALL LINE-UP, J.R. IT'S FULL OF SIMPLE-MINDED STORY LINES, VIOLENCE AND SEXUAL INNUENDOS, IT SHOULD BE A GREAT SEASON!"

# An offer they can't refuse

Two letters to two editors of different publications caught my eye this week.

One, to the editor of *Time* magazine from a New Hampshire woman said, "I prefer the 'silent scream' of the unwanted fetus to the reverberating cry of the unwanted child."

The other letter was to the editor of *The Washington Post*. A woman in Maryland wrote, "...there is no greater crime than a child who is unloved, unwanted or abused." Yes there is. It is the child who is killed. A live child at least has hope that if his biological parents don't love him, want him, or treat him right, someone will someday. A dead child has no such hope at all.

But this is not another discourse on all too familiar arguments for and against abortion. It is, instead, an examination of what has come to be known as the "unwanted child" justification for abortion. When one cannot win on the merits, one can create an unprovable premise.

Leaving aside the rejoinder that abortion-on-demand has failed to eliminate child abuse or create an environment in which only those children who are wanted and loved may live, as its advocates claimed it would, what must be said of those who assert that abortion must be preserved in order to form a more perfect family union?

Are some abortion advocates so selfish and presumptuous that they believe just because they might not want the child, no one else does? Does our disdain for what is on our dinner plates mean that a starving Ethiopian would not relish it?

We know from a number of quarters that there are as many people waiting to adopt children as there are women aborting them, so why are such children deemed "unwanted"? My own children may be unwanted to others, but they are very much wanted by me. Were the situation reversed, would I then be justified in snuffing out their lives? Is the value of a child assigned or is it unalienable?

As the battle over abortion rages on television and in newspaper stories, a quiet but remarkable development is sweeping the country. Thousands of people are opening their homes to women and girls "in trouble," as they used to say. More organized crisis pregnancy centers are also springing up. As recently as five years ago, such places, which included the old Florence

Crittenton homes, were shutting down as remnants of a bygone era. Birth control and abortion, coupled with the easing of the social stigma attached to out-of-wedlock pregnancies, had caused the homes to go the way of the wringer washer.

Dr. Jack Wilke, president of National Right to Life, says there are now nearly 4,000 "helping centers" across the country, reaching out to women who are pregnant and in need of help. He says the number is growing.

One such home was started by Monroe and Lois Whitehead in Tupelo, Mississippi. They wrote me about it. Funding for the home comes from private donations and the women are admitted without regard to race, religion, or marital status. A seventy-six-year-old woman volunteers her time, helping the mostly young women learn skills they can use when they leave. Monroe Whitehead says he treats the women as "guests" in his home because he cares. So who's unwanted?

Dr. William Pierce, president of the National Committee on Adoption, says there are now fifty maternity homes under development. He estimates there are "tens of thousands" of homes like the Whiteheads' and that the growth appears to be spontaneous with no one organization responsible for the increase, though many are contributing to it.

There are not nearly enough of these homes and centers, but there are sufficient numbers for me to make an offer that no woman facing a crisis pregnancy should be able to refuse. If you or someone you know would keep her baby rather than abort it if she had a place to live or wishes to exercise the adoption option but does not know where to turn, write me and I'll put you in touch with one of these places where there is no such thing as an "unwanted baby."

The most callous statement on abortion I have ever read came from the New York City Chapter of the National Organization for Women. In responding to a new law requiring places that sell liquor to post warning signs about the possible hazards to unborn babies, the NOW statement said, "We are most uneasy about the step this legislation takes toward protecting the unborn at the expense of women's freedom."

Unwanted babies? Maybe to NOW, but I prefer to call the adults "unwilling parents."

# Decadence

When one is six feet seven inches tall and crammed into the coach section of a transatlantic flight between London and Washington, one does not have many choices for diversion. He can either read, watch the movie, or talk to the person next to him. The movie sounded boring, I had read the airline magazine through twice, and the only remaining option was to talk to the distinguished older woman sitting next to me.

She was on her way to Washington, D.C. to visit her daughter, son-in-law, and grandchildren. She said that she always enjoyed coming to America. There was something about the country that she found invigorating.

Unaccustomed to hearing praise for America from abroad, I inquired, with some reservations, what that invigorating quality might be.

She said that in Britain there is too much cynicism and a feeling that no matter how hard one works, it does not make any difference because there will always be someone who is pushing you down. In America, she said, things are so much different. She said that in America one gets the feeling that "the dream" lives, that if one works hard enough and believes in the dream, one can achieve almost anything.

Now I know what Sally Field meant when she said at the Academy Awards, "You like me. You like me!" Oh-oh-oh-oh, what a feeling!

The immaculately dressed woman spoke of the "dynamic spirit" that is alive in America and how it always gives her a special thrill to come here.

I asked her why she thinks her country is so cynical.

She responded with a word I had not heard used for some time: decadence. "Britain is so decadent," she said.

Webster defines decadence this way: "marked by decay or decline." A synonym is offered. It is "deterioration."

If one agrees that Britain is decadent, is it really that far removed from the condition of the United States? Only in degree, I think. Decadence is always preceded by gross self-indulgence and worship of the god of materialism.

The now defunct *New Times* magazine published an essay on decadence before it folded in January 1979. It is somewhat dated, but the power of the message is still there. The essay said in part: "Welcome to

"HEY, I KNOW HOW WE CAN SHUT THEM DOWN ... LET'S TELL THE SUPREME COURT THE DANCERS ALWAYS OPEN THEIR ACT WITH PRAYER!"

America...C'mon in. Something for every palate. Reproductions by Rockefeller. Senators by David Garth, exploding Pintos by Ford...Carcinogens in 31 flavors. Opium from Saint Laurent, Seconals from Graceland...funky, punky, junky...you want it, we got it...

"There's something in the air—a sense of slippage, the perfume of decay. Life is slick and bright and noisy, but there's a softness here, a crumbling behind the gloss...There are almost no famous people anymore, only celebrities—'personalities'—Fame is passé. It is much too solid, too suggestive of steady achievement. There are ripples of grace and distinction, commitment and courage, but all seem in shorter supply now. It's no time for heroes..."

As the good economic news continues to cascade down from on high (the government, that is), we would do well to remember that very little stands between us and what the distinguished lady next to me on the plane labeled the decadence of once Great Britain.

A tolerance for what used to be intolerable is not maturity but self-centeredness. An endorsement of the decline in the value of human life through abortion and infanticide is not growth toward freedom but retreat toward bondage. Using money and the growth in the personal income of some as the yardstick for national health is not renewal, but decay. Have we forgotten that the love of money is the root of all evil? Can the operation be a success if the patient's vital moral signs can no longer be measured?

The Administration sometimes overemphasizes the economy, wishing we would not notice that underneath it all is a sense of slippage, a softness, a crumbling behind the gloss. All the missiles we can make will not be enough to defend us against *this* enemy. The British lady only sees the gloss. Those who live here see more and more of the underside and wonder that if decadence has enveloped Britain, can it be long before we are caught in its chilling embrace?

"NO, NO, MADAM, I SAID JESUS SAT DOWN AND ATE WITH PUBLICANS... NOT REPUBLICANS!"

# Tarring fundamentalists

One sees the word everywhere. Without exception its connection is always negative. Fundamentalism, like McCarthyism, like Orwellian, has taken on a life of its own. It is used to describe the extreme, the bizarre. It is something to be avoided, like unclean service station rest rooms.

The word has been badly misused and, as a result, misunderstood (William Safire, are you listening?). The dictionary, to which all honest writers must repair for proper definitions, says fundamentalism is "a movement in twentieth century Protestantism emphasizing the literally interpreted Bible as fundamental to Christian life and teaching." Leaving aside the theological ramifications of whether God had enough strength left after creating the universe to cause puny humankind to write words accurately on paper, what does this definition say about the misuse of the word *fundamentalism* in most news stories?

*The Post* tells us in the headline of a recent front-page story that "Islamic Fundamentalism Surges." The copy says this "fundamentalism" is "reflected in Lebanon's spreading civil warfare and the terrorist explosions in Kuwait."

But *The Post* isn't alone in its etymological heresy. *USA Today,* March 11, 1983, under the headline, "Dad Blamed for Death," says this: "Henry Morgan, 32, a fundamentalist from Oberlin, Ohio, was convicted Thursday of involuntary manslaughter in the starvation death of his 3-year-old daughter. Morgan at first refused to testify, saying he answers 'only to Jesus.' 'I don't understand your laws. I don't know anything but Jesus,' Morgan told his defense laywer..."

Can one imagine a slightly different story that begins: "Marvin Schwartz, 32, an Orthodox Jew from New York City, was convicted Thursday of involuntary manslaughter in the starvation death of his 3-year-old daughter. Schwartz said he didn't understand any laws but the laws of the Old Testament." One can imagine no such thing.

Subliminally, this misuse of the word *fundamentalism* sullies those to whom fundamentalism has a positive connotation but who are hopelessly stereotyped because the word has fallen into disrepute.

Why are fundamentalists never perceived as doing anything good? It is because the perceivers—journalists—cannot see beyond their own prejudices. Why are fundamentalists never portrayed operating soup kitchens or free food and clothing stores for the poor? They do. Why is the image of fundamentalists almost always that (in America, at least) of a polyester-suit, white-socks, burr-haircut, American-flag-tie, lapel-pin, gum-chewing, white person who barely graduated from high school, has a paneled recreation room with a National Rifle Association certificate in a K-Mart frame, and drives a pickup truck with a gun rack and a "Jesus Saves" bumper sticker on the rear?

There will always be just enough stereotypes to justify bigotry (ask blacks, Poles, Italians, Roman Catholics, Jewish persons, etc.). But the ignorant, I would even say deliberate, misuse of the word *fundamentalism* does a disservice to the public and to fundamentalists alike.

When black Americans sought to be identified as "blacks" instead of "Negroes" as had been the case for so many years, reporters were quick to grant them the right to be called what they liked. When homosexuals preferred "gay" to other labels, they, too, were granted that right. So why can't fundamentalists in America be accurately defined and described? Why must they bear the slur of being identified with bombings in Lebanon and Kuwait? Not all fundamentalists are the same. They should not be identified as a one-dimensional class any more than should blacks or women or any other people with certain things in common.

The late Egyptian President Anwar Sadat once remarked that the Ayatollah Khomeini was not a true Moslem, but a "fanatic." Fundamentalism does not translate into "fanaticism," though some fundamentalists are fanatics. But so are some nonfundamentalists and so are some nonreligious people and so are most "fans" of the Washington Redskins. So what does that prove?

I wonder how long I will have to wait for an explanation from the television weather persons as to what "inches of mercury" means when describing barometric readings and, for that matter, what that information is supposed to tell me? Similarly, I wonder when reporters who use and misuse the word *fundamentalism* will tell me what they mean by that so I will know, as they say in California, "where they are coming from." Is it too much to ask journalists to define their terms and to use the right word in the right place? I think not.

# The CBS takeover bid

Regardless of whether Ted Turner succeeds in his bid to acquire CBS, the public will be the eventual beneficiary.

A rare X-ray of the CBS mindset has allowed the public eye to see the incredible arrogance and elitist attitude which has served to turn so many Americans against the press.

If you are fortunate enough to have cable in your area, you may have seen some of the extended coverage of the CBS stockholder's meeting in Chicago.

CBS board chairman Thomas Wyman said with a straight face that if the network is taken over, it would be bad for the Constitution and terrible for the country.

Can he be serious? Is the corporate welfare of CBS to be equated with the future of America? These guys are so puffed up with a sense of their own importance that someone should paint the name "Goodyear" on their backsides and float them over football stadiums.

The statement I liked best, though, was Wyman's response to a woman stockholder, who asked whether he believed Turner is "moral" enough to run a network. Wyman said he did not think so. It is this "holier than thou" attitude that is part of the arrogance problem.

No one ever suggested that Ted Turner is a candidate for sainthood, but at least he runs "Leave it to Beaver," while CBS is engaged in other pursuits.

Does CBS seriously consider itself to be moral, and therefore immune from takeover, when it owns 50 percent of Playboy's Rainbow Programming Service as well as the distribution rights to Playboy's videocassettes?

According to The National Federation for Decency, a media watchdog group, CBS has no leg to stand on if it wants to claim a higher moral ground than Ted Turner. Recent plot outlines of CBS programs include a Catholic prostitute, a transexual, occasional profanity, and children perusing pornographic magazines ("The World According to Garp"); two divorced women and their two lesbian friends agree that a family is any group of people who love each other and want to share their lives together ("Kate and Allie"); and antichurch bigotry, the opposition of traditional moral values, and the promotion of sexual promiscuity ("Mistral's Daughter," of which television writer John O'Connor said, "(it) retains all of the . . . vulgar fantasy that has become the (Judith) Krantz trademark in

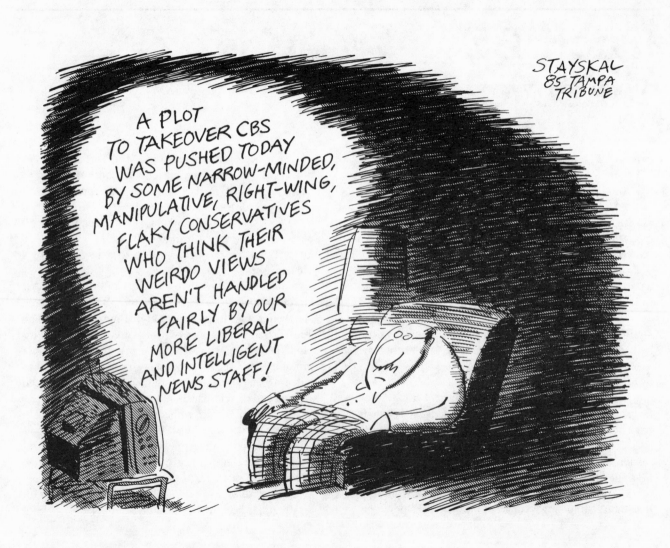

such previous works as 'Scruples' and 'Princess Daisy'").

The list goes on and includes the CBS movie "Passions," which featured a minister whose wife and twenty-year-old daughter made up one family and whose mistress of eight years, who had a six-year-old son fathered by him, made up the other. If morality were the test that determined whether the current crew remained in control at CBS, then the corporate litmus paper would turn the color of green slime.

"Entertainment" programming aside, CBS News has come in for particularly strong criticism because of its perceived arrogance.

The arrogance factor was dealt with in a remarkably frank and unusually well-balanced program on ABC called "Viewpoint." Media critic Jeff Greenfield spoke of the supposed "constitutional mandate of the press." Greenfield was challenged by *National Review* publisher William Rusher, who asserted that "the Constitution of the United States says that any of us, to the extent that we have anything to say, have within certain broad limits the right to say it. That's all. There's no mandate given to the press to behave in any particular way . . . We are all equal."

It is a delicious irony that CBS, which continues to pay Dan Rather's inflated salary, once broadcast reports by Rather in which he scathed Richard Nixon for "stonewalling" and refusing to acknowledge guilt in the Watergate caper. Now that the shoe is on the other foot, CBS refuses to admit that it makes mistakes and gets huffy when many American suggest it is not infallible.

ABC's Ted Koppel displayed the evenhandedness that has made him the fairest network journalist in America when he summed up the "Viewpoint" program this way: "We in the media do have a distressing habit of forgetting or ignoring the fact that the skeptic's privilege to criticize also carries with it the responsibility of getting it right, of being accurate. Too often we respond to complaints against our methods by waving the First Amendment at our critics as though it was some sacred totem that endows all who pay it homage with infallibility." In case you didn't recognize it, that's humility, which is in too short supply in the press. It's absence is what is fueling the takeover fires.

Were more journalists cast in Ted Koppel's mold, perhaps we would not see the press held in such low esteem. Perhaps the other Ted ought to be buying CBS.

STAYSKAL
84 TAMPA
TRIBUNE

# Day-care concerns

There was shocking testimony delivered last week before two congressional subcommittees on day-care programs.

Kee MacFarlane, a nationally recognized expert in the treatment of sexually abused children, told the congressmen she suspects a "child predators" network is operating in this country and, although the evidence is circumstantial, that a conspiracy exists to operate day-care centers as a cover for child pornography. MacFarlane testified she personally knows of hundreds of children who have alleged they were pornographically photographed during their entire time at preschools and that some children were transported to other towns where the photographs were made.

While acknowledging that the vast majority of child sexual abuse does not emanate from preschools, MacFarlane raises an issue that most people would just as soon ignore. Those engaged in the sexual exploitation of children are counting on the public not to pay attention to the problem.

Despite occasional publicity, there exists among the public a "see no evil" mentality about this form of child abuse, which is just fine with two of the better organized pedophile societies: the North American Man/Boy Love Association (NAMBLA) and the more radical René Guyon Society, whose crude slogan is, "sex before eight, or else it's too late."

The stated objective of NAMBLA is outlined in one of its brochures: "We oppose age-of-consent laws and other legislation against the freedom of youth." It has been alleged that NAMBLA and related organizations, such as The British Pedophile Information Exchange (PIE), which wants the age of consent dropped as low as four, operate or are aware of an international network that provides information to men about young boys who are available for sexual encounters.

It is estimated that the physical abuse of children affects more than two million youngsters annually. Many of these cases involve sexual abuse.

Odyssey Institute, a New York-based organization which monitors sexual abuse of children and has been active in lobbying for tougher state and federal laws to deal with the problem, says child sexploitation has created a massive multibillion dollar market in the United States and throughout the world. This industry involves the use of children as young as three (and some younger) in the production of pornographic films and magazines and also in prostitution.

NAMBLA members are not the stereotype of the "dirty old man." Most are highly educated. Some are physicians, lawyers, social workers, or teachers. An estimated 80 percent were themselves the victims of sexual abuse as children. Some, of course, are pornographers, dedicated to making a lot of money at the expense of someone else's life. So much for the contention that pornography is a "victimless crime."

As Odyssey Institute President Dr. Judienne Densen-Gerber has noted, "Common sense and maternal instinct tell me that these abuses are not a question of freedom of speech and press. Children are not consenting adults; they are victims whose spirits are mutilated as their bodies are violated. This is a matter of child abuse and should be dealt with through child-abuse laws."

As state and local authorities investigate some of the more celebrated child abuse cases in day-care centers in New York and California, Congress should seriously consider various proposals to make sure such places cannot be used to sexually exploit vulnerable children. Under study are proposals that would establish stricter licensing requirements, improve monitoring systems with surprise visits, thoroughly check prospective employees, provide training for staff, board members, and parents, offer higher pay for day-care personnel, and develop sensitive ways of dealing with children in court.

It is traumatic enough for many parents to leave their children with strangers while they work. They should at least expect protection from the kind of predators who have turned the sexual abuse of children into a growth, or should I say "gross," industry.

# Censorship revisited

Certain intolerant, antiacademic freedom underminers of the First Amendment on the right cannot allow their children to be exposed to any ideas but their own. We are asked to believe that these rightists, usually of a religious bent, wish to unconstitutionally impose their world view on impressionable young people.

I have long suspected, however, that the real issue is not academic freedom, but academic control. An incident at Washington-Lee High School in Arlington, Virginia proves the point.

Guy Cavallo teaches psychology at Washington-Lee. One of his students brought him a copy of the pro-life film "The Silent Scream," which shows a computer-enhanced suction abortion, and asked him to show it to the class. The film, which has been shown in whole or in part on several networks, was screened by Cavallo, who decided it was too sensitive to present during school. Cavallo scheduled an after-school showing for students who wished to see it. The only condition, required by the school principal, was that students bring a signed permission slip from home.

When the parents of some students who did not want their children to see the film after school complained about other children seeing it, even with their parents' permission, the principal canceled the showing.

What does this tell us about tolerance and academic freedom? Sure, the film is controversial in the sense that many proabortionists do not like to confront what actually occurs during an abortion, but so what? Controversy never bothers those who wish to push liberal views of sex or nuclear weapons on students. In fact, those views are usually presented in class, with or without parental consent.

Take a case in Red Lion, Pennsylvania, for example. Testimony by students at a school board meeting alleged that a female instructor, who teaches sex education and coaches the girls swim team, authorized and conducted nude swims in the school swimming pool which is open to outside observers; conducted parties for the swim team at which she accepted sexually-oriented gifts from students; instructed students that a homosexual relationship was better than a heterosexual one; encouraged sex before marriage in a co-ed class of minor students; discussed oral sex in detail; and belittled parental authority.

"WE'RE NOT INSTILLING GOOD CHARACTER TRAITS IN KIDS?! BUT WE GOT RID OF EVERYTHING THAT WOULD HURT THEIR LITTLE MINDS... PRAYER, CREATION SCIENCE AND BIBLE STUDIES!"

Two years ago the National Education Association published a manual called "Choices: A Unit on Conflict and Nuclear War" for use during school hours. It was so heavily weighted in favor of a nuclear freeze that a teacher's union called it "propaganda."

Many liberals unapologetically promote their views in public school textbooks, including Theodore H. Von Laue, who told reporter John Lofton he did not include material on Communist atrocities in a recent history book published by Houghton Mifflin Company because, as a Quaker pacifist, he is "afraid of raising the temperature of indignation," on the theory that it leads to bad ends in our contemporary world. Von Laue worries that our children might build up a "hostility" toward communism "without understanding why these things happen."

One final example should suffice to convince all but the most biased reader of who is censoring whom.

Last month at Jamestown, Pennsylvania High School, fifty-three children in the American Culture class were subjected to someone's idea of a good lesson on the "dangers" of the continued defense buildup. Over the intercom came an announcement that school would be dismissed early because the Soviet Union had attacked an American ship and the President was about to address the nation. It was not true.

The experiment backfired. One student went into shock. Another started crying. Most sat in stunned silence, fearing that nuclear missiles were on the way.

Nobody asked that parental permission be obtained before subjecting the kids to this experiment. Neither was parental approval sought for the content of the sex education class or the extracurricular activities involving the girls swim team or the school textbook censorship or any of a long list of other academic idiocies.

But let a psychology teacher offer a film with a viewpoint other than the trendy one and you see just how far academic freedom extends.

This, of course, has nothing to do with academic freedom at all. It has a lot to do with intolerance and censorship of the grossest sort and it ought to be labeled just that.

# In Hollywood, religion is for nerds

The time was not long ago when indignant network television executives boldly said that no special-interest group was going to act as a censor or dictate the content of their programming. No siree! Not unless, that is, those special-interest groups hold to a particular world view with which the executives happen to agree. What a difference the right cause makes.

Take the recently aired movie, "Consenting Adult." ABC and the producers really outdid themselves on this one. Not only did the producers stay in regular touch with the homosexual community to make sure that every potential stereotype was avoided (and reality, too), but the *Los Angeles Times* carried two stories on the movie that made it appear to be the sexual equivalent of "The Autobiography of Miss Jane Pittman."

Consultants are very important to those with liberal tendencies. They help them justify their prejudices. There is no shortage of consultants when it comes to homosexual themes or nuclear disarmament. NBC employs a black Harvard professor to make sure that nothing in Bill Cosby's show smacks of "Amos 'n Andy."

When it comes to other themes—religion, for example—it's "Don't call us, and we won't call you." In the same editions of *The Times* that carried the stories on "Consenting Adult" there was an ad for a new movie called "Heaven Help Us." Says the ad copy: "If God had wanted them to be angels, He would have given them wings. The Brothers of St. Basil's School preach against vice, lust and disrespect. But that never stopped these guys." Neither did it stop the Hollywood producers, whose view of religion (and particularly the Catholic Church) is that it is far more dangerous to your system than a venereal disease.

Religion, Hollywood-style, is something for nerds and weirdos. While allowances can be made for those forced by parents to attend private schools, one is relegated to the ranks of the philosophic untouchables should he tarry a single day beyond his first opportunity to escape. "Mass Appeal," "The Thorn Birds"—all of them take the same dim view of religion, religious leaders, and those dumb enough to think that anything other than this life matters.

Michael Schwartz, director of the Catholic League

for Religious and Civil Rights in Milwaukee, says that producers will often hire a priest as a "technical consultant," but his role is "to make sure the vestments are straight and the Latin is correct. Never to my knowledge have they brought in a consultant to comment on the themes and stereotypes that are portrayed."

Schwartz faults Hollywood for being so far removed from reality that it does not think there are real people for whom faith is relevant in their everyday lives. He believes that producers view going to church or synagogue as something that people did long ago, but no longer. For them, he says, "Hollywood Wives" represents their statement of reality.

In a recent column in the *Wall Street Journal,* novelist and commentator Ben Stein says that, despite evidence of strong religious interest and practice, "there is virtually no appearance of religion at all (on prime-time television). Whenever a problem requiring moral judgment appears—which is on almost every show—the response that comes is based upon some intuitive knowledge of what is good and evil, the advice of a friend, a remembered counsel or, more likely, the invisible hand of circumstance . . . The good people do what is right and the bad people do what is wrong by some kind of secular compass. No one in prime time ever talks about religion as a guide in his own life."

Stein correctly sums up the reason for the absence of relevant religion on TV (and by extension in movies) when he observes, "It has something to do with network skittishness, and something to do with politics."

# Conversion

Lew Lehrman, who would be Governor of New York had Mario Cuomo not edged him out, has been converted. Lehrman, who once headed the Rite-Aid drug chain, and now heads a political organization called Citizens for America, was a Jew. He was recently baptized into the Roman Catholic Church at St. Thomas Moore's in New York.

What is even more interesting than the conversion itself is the reaction to it.

David Garth, a veteran Democratic political consultant who makes his living manufacturing United States Senators for sale to the public, said Lehrman's conversion could be more damaging to his political career than if he were divorced. Huh?

"Conversion is so much more unusual (than divorce)," Garth was quoted as saying. "It's a question of how he rationalizes it."

I guess that takes care of the critics who say Lehrman joined the Catholic Church for political reasons. If he was really interested only in politics, he would have divorced his wife.

Another political consultant, Robert Squier, said Lehrman's conversion "is about on a par with divorce," adding: "It can be handled in our time, but it probably couldn't have been handled a generation ago."

Actually, it is divorce that could not have been handled a generation ago. Squier has things mixed up. As recently as Nelson Rockefeller, a divorce automatically disqualified a person from becoming President in the minds of many. Now we have had a President whose wife was divorced (Gerald Ford) and a President who himself is divorced (Ronald Reagan). Conversion, on the other hand, found greater approval among members of the last generation.

The last major political figure to announce his conversion was former Nixon aide Charles Colson. I called him to learn what he made of the reaction to Lehrman's conversion. Why, I wanted to know, do some people respond to such stories with so much skepticism?

Colson believes there are three reasons. First, he says, many people believe that when a public figure is converted, he is doing it for self-gain. In his own case, this reason was quickly dispelled when Colson was sentenced to one to three years in prison for his role in the Watergate affair.

Second, Colson says many observers who have not

"HEY, NO PRAYING HERE ... THIS IS A PUBLIC BEACH!"

had a similar experience have difficulty in reconciling their own relationship with God. They believe that religion is something for backwoods people, but not for the educated and sophisticated. Conversions by learned people (Colson was an honors graduate and has an earned law degree, and Lehrman is no dummy, either) mystify and threaten them.

Third, the "unconverted" know little about the nature of true conversion because their only exposure to religion has come in its tainted form. They have seen the prosperity gospel or certain television preachers that turn them off with hucksterism and hypocrisy. When they witness the "real thing," they are unable to comprehend it.

I telephoned Lew Lehrman, hoping for an interview. He refused. He said he had turned down *Time* and *Newsweek,* both of which wanted to do a feature story, and that he did not want to talk about it. "To me, it is a private matter," he said. Doesn't sound to me like the type of guy who is looking to make political hay out of his conversion.

Charles Colson added a postscript to his thoughts on why some people find it difficult to accept a genuine conversion.

"The unbelieving world," he said, "cannot believe one is converted unless they believe in a Converter. Among the fashionable set, the white wine and Brie crowd, you're not 'with it' if you are converted.

When one of their own finds God, it drives the rest of them to the depths of despair, and the only way they can climb out of that despair is by analyzing the conversion from a political perspective or by denying its existential nature."

The truth, we are promised, is supposed to set us free. Now that Lew Lehrman believes he has found the truth, it is to be hoped that he will not be put in bondage by those who, as Charles Colson put it, do not enjoy a similar experience.

"I HAD THAT ONE ABORTED!"

# Baby seals and abortion

The author of the Chinese proverb knew what he was talking about when he said, "One picture is worth more than 10,000 words."

Last week the mail brought a letter from the International Fund for Animal Welfare. Accompanying the letter was a folded poster. On the outside of the poster were these words: "CAUTION: The photos displayed on this miniposter show scenes of Canadian fishermen killing seals. You will find them extremely disturbing." And so I did, but not just for the reasons the animal welfare people think.

Inside were graphic color pictures of baby harp seals, their heads bloodied by the seal hunters, who were "harvesting" their crop for the special few who can afford coats made from their pelts.

Accompanying the pictures of the bloodied seals was a letter which called for a boycott of Canadian fish until this "nauseating carnage" and "inhuman" treatment of seals stop.

Since the seals are not human, the "inhumanity" I am asked to oppose must involve the behavior of the human seal hunters.

The graphic and moving depiction of a seal harvest causes me to wonder why we have not been exposed to pictures of aborted baby humans. Abortion occurs at a rate nearly ten times that of the killing of baby seals. Like the seal harvests, abortion has been turned into a "growth" industry.

Attempts by prolife groups to show pictures of what happens during an abortion have been rebuffed by the commercial networks and nearly all local stations because the pictures do not show "the other side" (is there a concern for the "other side" in seal hunting?). Yet, for those who are opposed to abortion, the "other side" to their position is all that has been seen. Allowing this one-sided presentation to continue does not offer women a choice at all. The very word *choice* presupposes freedom of access to information so the choice will be an informed one.

In every case where those who oppose abortion have sought to enact laws that would give a woman more information about the nature of the life within her, about alternatives to abortion and about what occurs during an abortion, the so-called "prochoicers" have rebuffed them. Yet these are some of the same people who defend free speech, academic freedom, and the public's right to know.

There is a new film that makes the best case yet for the prolife position. The film is "Conceived in Liberty." Unlike material from the prochoicers, this film contains arguments from both sides. Abortion doctors defend "the right to choose" in more than token appearances. But it is the pictures which speak "10,000 words."

The film focuses on those 17,000 babies discovered two years ago in a container in a Los Angeles suburb. A tough-as-nails truck driver looked at the products of abortion, and he nearly cries as he tells what he saw.

Most of us will never have that opportunity unless we order the film through National Right to Life in Washington, D.C. But shouldn't we be permitted to see pictures like these if we are to be persuaded that the Supreme Court was right when it ushered in abortion-on-demand? Shouldn't concepts behind "truth in packaging" laws and the Freedom of Information Act be extended to abortion?

If the argument is that the pictures are too emotional, what about the seal pictures, or the pictures of blacks being beaten by clubs and bitten by dogs in the sixties, or of Jews in the death-camps of Nazi Germany, or more recently of dead Palestinians and dead Americans lying in the streets of Lebanon and transmitted into our dinner hours via satellite? Emotions are part of our human makeup.

To deny an appeal to emotions in the abortion of humans while appealing to them in the clubbing of seals is dishonest and forces women to make decisions without having all the facts.

# The latest in school reading

Twenty-five years ago, when I was in high school, some of us used to hide a copy of *Peyton Place* or *Blackboard Jungle* inside our literature book. The English teacher wondered why we did so poorly on tests despite such obvious classroom dedication to the "assigned material."

Just as attempts to hide prohibited gum under our tongues would inevitably be discovered, so too would our deception with the unassigned books, which would be taken away, probably, we thought, to be read later by the teacher or the vice principal.

Now our own kids are in school and a lot of us are wondering whatever became of the old standards and the presumption that certain books were good for us and others were to be avoided, at least until we achieved greater maturity.

The November issue of *English Journal,* a publication of the National Council of Teachers of English, shows how far things have gone. The publication, which goes to thousands of public school teachers throughout the country, carries an article which recommends homosexual literature for junior and senior high school students.

The author, David E. Wilson, teaches at Kirkwood Community College in Cedar Rapids, Iowa. The article contains a bibliography of fiction and nonfiction books on homosexuality with such titles as, *Out of the Closet, But Paying the Price: Lesbian and Gay Characters in Children's Literature* (reviewed by the Interracial Books for Children Bulletin, a federally funded organization), and *Almost Grown and Gay,* along with a series of books specifically targeted for lesbians and homosexual males as young as the seventh grade.

Mr. Wilson repeats the standard line of homosexual advocates, that 10 percent of the country is "gay," therefore one out of ten kids in junior and senior high must be homosexual, therefore let's make sure they get books which offer encouragement in that lifestyle and the "positive role models" they need.

Says Mr. Wilson, "These kids are often afraid, confused, and curious about their sexual identities. They wonder how others handled similar feelings, but they're afraid to ask." Mr. Wilson not only wants them to ask, he is pushing books that will give them the answers he wants them to have.

Seven homosexual books for "young adults" are

"HEY, LOOK ... JUST LIKE WE HAD IN SEX EDUCATION TODAY!"

STAYSKAL
84 CHICAGO
TRIBUNE

reviewed by Mr. Wilson, including *Dance on My Grave,* by Aidan Chambers: sixteen-year-old Hal Robinson is looking for the perfect friendship when along comes Barry Gorman. The two boys quickly become buddies, then lovers, and Hal learns what it means to be committed to someone else. In the end, Barry dies a violent death and we are told, "Fortunately Hal grows from the experience and does not betray himself by denying his homosexuality." Whew! That would have been a tragedy.

Or how about *Independence Day,* by B. A. Ecker? It is about Mike Ramsay, "a popular 15-year-old soccer player with an attractive girlfriend, an understanding best friend, and a close family. He also has a problem: he's beginning to realize he is gay and in love with his best friend, who is not."

Other recommended books for homosexual boys and girls include *A Boy's Own Story, Annie on My Mind, Young, Gay and Proud* and *One Teenager in Ten,* in which "Eleven women and 17 men talk about their coming out experiences. The authors, all from the United States and Canada, range in age from 15 to 24."

Wilson writes, "Still more books with healthy, happy homosexual characters need to be written, published, and made available to young adults . . . homosexuality must be presented as (a visible) and real alternative to heterosexuality."

The problem with this line of thinking and with books that advocate that heterosexuals "do their own thing" is that it goes against what many parents are trying their best to teach at home. Parents are already up against formidable odds, given the heavy sexual content of television, movies, and hard rock music. They hardly need additional grief, particularly when it is subsidized with their own tax money.

Curious, isn't it? Mr. Wilson probably would advocate that religion and religious values have no place in the public schools, but should be taught at home, or in church or synagogue. Yet he openly advocates books for "young adults" (a seventh-grader is a young adult?) that teach values anathema to religious and nonreligious alike.

Maybe somebody ought to bring this up at the next PTA meeting.

# Mayor Barry and the bombings

The mayor of Washington, D.C., Marion Barry, has called the bombing of abortion clinics, "terrorist acts," comparable to the Nazis and the Ku Klux Klan. Leaving aside the argument that the Nazis and the Klan killed people and the anti-abortionists say their goal in bombing buildings is to prevent the destruction of innocent human life, let us press on to analyze the mayor's analogy. Even better, let us observe the position of the mayor and his fellow civil rights activists twenty years ago when violence against people and buildings was coming from the left and not the right.

In the middle 1960s, young Marion Barry headed the Washington chapter of the Student Non-Violent Coordinating Committee (SNCC). Following the assassination of Dr. Martin Luther King, Jr., SNCC's national chairman, Stokely Charmichael, was reported by the *Evening Star* to have said, "King's death made it a lot easier for a lot of Negroes—they know it's time to get guns now."

Some believe it was remarks like that which contributed to the riots in cities across America. Five hundred and ninety-five fires were set across the country follow-ing King's death, and Stokely Charmichael observed, "That was light stuff compared with what is about to happen."

Try as I might, I was unable to find a single news-paper story from that period which reported Marion Barry as having denounced Charmichael's inflammatory rhetoric or the riots.

While King and other prominent black leaders eschewed violence and made nonviolence the corner-stone of the civil rights movement, still others moved in a more violent direction.

In their book, *Cities Under Siege: An Anatomy of Ghetto Riots, 1964-1968* (Basic Books, 1971), David Baisel and Peter H. Rossi resurrect some interesting quotes from blacks who are today held in high esteem as precursors to the nonviolent wing of the civil rights movement.

In the chapter "Black Violence in the Twentieth Century: A Study in Rhetoric and Retaliation," the authors quote Robert Williams, former president of the Monroe, North Carolina branch of the NAACP, who said, "Our only logical and successful answer is to meet organized and massive violence with massive and organized violence . . ."

W. E. B. DuBois, the noted protest leader and a founder of the NAACP, occasionally 35vocated retaliatory violence. In 1916 DuBois admonished black youth to stop shouting platitudes of accommodation and remember that no people ever achieved liberation without an armed struggle.

Remember when violence was more trendy? Remember when the Berrigan brothers destroyed federal property because of the "immorality" of the Vietnam war and the arms race?

What about *The New York Review of Books* which in the midsixties featured a Molotov cocktail on its cover and the recipe inside. *The Review* said America was reaching the point where revolution was morally required. Who denounced that philosophy? Not Marion Barry.

Of Mayor Barry's attempt to link the abortion clinic bombers to the Nazis, theologian Carl F. H. Henry says that the Nazis "repudiated an objective moral order which denied the universal dignity of man." Henry says the Nazis stressed Nordic superiority and Jewish inferiority much as the proabortionists (excuse me . . . prochoicers) stress the inferiority of unborn babies and the KKK the inferiority of blacks.

As to the morality of blowing up abortion clinics, that is a more difficult challenge. Richard John Neuhaus of the Center for Religion and Society in New York put the question correctly in a book called *Movement and Revolution* (Doubleday, 1970).

Said Neuhaus of the violent antiwar and civil rights protestors of that day, "Do they mean to say that the time has come to declare this government morally illegitimate and in the name of a higher law say that it is legitimate and imperative to engage in violence to change policy?"

Neuhaus says there are such cases which demand revolution, but revolution must always be the last step. The question that must be asked today, he says, is whether the last step in the abortion debate has been reached.

If you want my opinion, I'm personally opposed to the bombings, but I wouldn't want to impose my morality on others.

# Sugar-free, substance-free Ferraro

Why are some commentators so upset about former Congressperson and Vice Presidential candidate Geraldine Ferraro accepting half a million bucks to sell Diet Pepsi? Columnist Ellen Goodman, a Ferraro booster, calls the deal a "sellout." Come, come. One must have something to sell in order to sell out. Having been rejected in forty-nine states along with Walter Mondale, Ferraro is joining the Pepsi generation to try another line of work.

We're not talking worth here. Worth is an entirely different matter. Of course Barbara Walters is not *worth* a million dollars anymore than Dan Rather is *worth* eight million. It's what you can get up front that counts, and hang the reviews.

Actually Ferraro is following a great tradition. Eleanor Roosevelt hawked margarine on TV. Gerald Ford and Henry Kissinger have played on "Dynasty," Alan Greenspan, former Chairman of the Council of Economic Advisers, is trying to sell you an Apple computer, Ronald Reagan sold GE in between political jobs, former North Carolina Senator Sam Ervin did American Express commercials, and Walter Mondale's speechwriter is leaving one Mickey Mouse operation for another one. Marty Kaplan is moving to Burbank to toil for Walt Disney Studios.

Those who are concerned about such things believe that moving from the public to the private trough demeans politics. Nonsense. It is because politics already has been demeaned that it leads to such "sellouts" as Geraldine Ferraro's Pepsi commercials and the attempt to grab all the financial gusto one can.

We make incredible demands on our public figures, demands that are almost hypocritical. We require them to conform to a standard many of us could not live up to. We demand that they be well-educated and have the kind of experience that would allow many of them to earn considerably more in private life. If they are in Congress, they must maintain two homes and incur other expenses that are unique to the job. Is it any wonder that so many in public life, Republicans and Democrats, liberals and conservatives, eagerly take the first jackpot offered them?

Actually, politicans and diet soda have a lot in common (stay with me now). It used to be that products were sold by what they contained. Today as we pursue

our narcissistic pleasures, many products are sold based on what they do not contain. Caffeine-free, sugar-free, salt-free sodas. Principle-free politicians.

In the diet sodas there is absolutely nothing that is nourishing. Taste is all you get. In a lot of politicians there is very little substance. Form is all you get. What's the difference?

Many politicians today have forgotten what leadership is all about. They stick their fingers in the wind in the form of campaign consultants and pollsters and they go whichever way they are told, rather than establishing a foundation based on principles and then leading their constituents in the right direction.

Where have all the leaders gone, long time passing?

Today survival is the name of the game. If economics is what the people want, economics is what they'll get. Never mind the so-called "social issues." Joseph Stalin didn't care about the moral force of the Pope ("How many divisions does the Pope have?") Most politicians don't give a rip about the unborn ("how many votes do the babies have?").

And so, on we go with the distinction between selling a product and the politician as product so blurred that few can remember where the demarcation line was once drawn.

Some time ago I was flying into Washington, D.C. from St. Louis. A woman across the aisle was trying to subdue her restless preschool daughter. Said the woman,

"Look out the window, honey, and see the beautiful lights of Washington."

The child was transfixed for a moment and then blurted out, "Mommy, mommy, it's Disneyland!" For her, there was no difference. Disneyland was fantasy without substance and Washington, from the air at least, looked the same.

"EAT YOUR DINNER, ARTHUR. DON'T YOU WANT TO GROW UP TO BE BIG AND STRONG LIKE YOUR MOTHER?"

# Sexual guerrillas in retreat

What is going on here? First, we have Betty Friedan, matriarch of the so-called "women's movement," going beyond the feminine mystique to endorse families and commitment in marriage.

Then Jane Fonda tells the "CBS Morning News" that she "made some mistakes" as a younger woman by going to Hanoi and speaking out against the war in the South and, in the minds of some of those demonstrating against her personal appearances these days, aiding and comforting the enemy.

Next, feminist columnist Ellen Goodman of the *Boston Globe* acknowledges that the Supreme Court's *Roe vs. Wade* decision in 1973 arbitrarily establishing twenty-eight weeks as the "viability" standard for the unborn ought to be pushed back in light of recent medical discoveries.

Then we encounter Germaine Greer, the Che Guevera of female sexuality, surveying all that she has unmade and declaring it not so very good.

Even "God-is-dead" theologian Harvey Cox of Harvard has discovered a pulse in the Deity after all and allowed that God, in fact, may not be dead. Perhaps He is only comatose, but His condition is improving.

While the Friedan, Goodman, Fonda, and Cox positions are interesting, what is positively fascinating is the admission by Germaine Greer in the April *Ms.* magazine that sexual guerrilla warfare has not lived up to its advance billing. Though Ms. Greer is a long way from any kind of conversion, her acknowledgment in the magazine article adapted from a new book, that doing it "her way" may not be in the best interest of women and young girls, is undoubtedly a long-overdue first step toward that end.

In copy loaded with multisyllabic words which make her appear the flipside of William F. Buckley Jr., Ms. Greer seems to be suggesting in no uncertain terms that the sexual revolution not only has failed to overthrow the established order, but that it has served to endorse that order as the better way, the better truth, and the better life.

To wit, "What if chastity is no more unnatural than lechery?"

And, "Perhaps the least questioned of all the assumptions underlying modern liberal attitudes is the assumption that chastity is an unnatural state, imposed upon the individual by repressive authorities, religion or parents or both and internalized to varying degrees as relative impotence.''

Or, ''Bad sex is unlike bad food in that it is worse than no food at all.''

Or, ''. . . it has become crushingly obvious that the condition of women under the permissive regime has deteriorated. Anyone in the confidence of young women asking for help cannot fail to be struck by the high price they are paying for what may very well be unsatisfactory sex . . . With a shock I hear my own voice saying to 14-year-olds, 'If it's resistible, don't do it. Better no sex than bad sex.' ''

Would that chastity might find its way into more sex education curricula. It solves so many problems and obviates the need for, among other things, antibiotics.

Who, pray tell, is responsible for young women ''in need of help'' because of their involvement in the land of ''do your own thingism''? This is where Ms. Greer's potential conversion breaks down because it must first be preceded by repentance.

Neither Greer, nor Friedan, nor Cox, nor Goodman will admit that he (or she) has made a mistake. In the shifting sands of nonabsolutes one is allowed to alter one's theory and move on. No matter that an entire generation has been damaged. No matter that lives of young women and men have been irreversibly scarred. Let us push on to the next theory, equally as bad. This can be accomplished because the social theorists are never called to account for their past sins. They change lifestyles as easily as they might change clothing or hairstyles.

What these people have opened by their frank admissions that the policies of the past have failed, is a window of vulnerability for them and a window of opportunity for those whose traditional values have been vindicated. Those who hold to the old values, however, must act quickly, before the window of opportunity is slammed shut. When opportunity knocks, one had better make sure he is at home to answer.

# The other side of consensus

In his speech at Notre Dame on religion and politics, New York Gov. Mario Cuomo said, in effect, that when there is a conflict between God and Caesar, his slogan (and ours) should be, "we have no king but Caesar."

While the governor is certainly correct in urging churches, synagogues, and their members to take a more active role in caring for people in need, his argument obscures an underlying philosophy, which is the autonomy of man. Such autonomy requires us to worship at the shrine of technology, science, and government, and believe that they alone can solve our problems. For those who lack ultimate faith in these institutions, the state is to impose such devotion. This is for our own good, of course.

Mr. Cuomo's central flaw, from which his other errors flow, is rooted in this one sentence: "We create our public morality through consensus and, in this country, that consensus reflects to some extent religious values of a great majority of Americans." This is autonomous man's declaration of independence from God, from absolutes, from everything but his own mind. It is also a claim not rooted in history.

In our century alone there are numerous examples. Prohibition did not enjoy a consensus. If it had, the bootleggers would not have flourished and the 18th Amendment would not have been repealed.

In 1954, when there was hardly a consensus on civil rights, the Supreme Court decided in *Brown vs. Board of Education* that "separate but equal" was not to be tolerated and that public schools would have to be desegregated "with all deliberate speed." Twenty-five years of civil unrest followed.

Was there a consensus in the early 1960s when the Supreme Court outlawed mandatory prayer and Bible reading in public schools? There was not. There is a consensus (more than 80 percent) who want voluntary prayer restored, but they are not getting it. It appears that consensus is a one-way street.

Did a consensus exist in 1973 when the Supreme Court overturned the laws of fifty states (were they passed in the first place by consensus?) and allowed abortion to the moment of live birth? It did not and it still does not today, but the law remains.

The danger in this illogic should be obvious. It was consensus that denied blacks their freedom and then their

civil rights. It was consensus that put Jews in the gas chambers and before firing squads. A god of consensus leads to situational ethics which has jeopardized, and may continue to jeopardize, people who find themselves on the short end of what the consensus happens to be at a given moment.

Mr. Cuomo said that "I protect my right to be a Catholic by preserving your right to believe as a Jew, a Protestant, or nonbeliever, or as anything else you choose." No, he doesn't. That right is protected because, in the words of Thomas Jefferson, it is an endowed, inalienable right, not granted by the institutions of men and women (which can take them away at any time) but by "our Creator." Does that compel men and women to worship or believe in that Creator? Certainly not. What it does is to put certain rights outside the reach of corrupt humankind.

Dr. F. G. Oosterhoff, former history professor at the University of Winnipeg, has observed, "People in our country and in other Western countries are often amazed at the government's lack of moral leadership, at its willingness to obey the demands of society (or of the majority of society, or even of a minority, as long as it is vocal enough and has managed to get control of the media), and to legalize these demands, no matter how preposterous they may be, and no matter how often they may change . . . If people are sovereign, rather than God, then their will is law. The absolute norms go, and the government as the servant of the people can only follow the ever changing whims of its masters, until finally the chaos is total, and the masters, in desperation, make their servant king and bow their heads under a tyrant's yoke."

# Memories

Ah, April! The promises it brings that if we endure the showers we can expect May flowers. And the memories it brings, too. Particularly this April, the tenth anniversary of the end in Indochina, where the dominoes fell, after all.

As a Heritage Foundation publication reminds us, it was on April 17, 1975, that the Khmer Rouge captured Phnom Penh, Cambodia. On April 30, North Vietnamese tanks rolled into Saigon, in violation of the Paris Peace agreements. On August 23, the Pathet Lao abandoned all pretense of a coalition government and seized the last domino in Laos.

What is remarkable about Indochina is not that the Communists failed to live up to the Paris peace accords ("we will bury you" supersedes all other promises), but that so many American politicians and commentators predicted a different outcome.

Examining the record is like discovering a fifty-year-old time capsule loaded with predictions for 1985, none of which came true. If it were not so tragic for the people of Indochina, these predictions would be funny.

On March 17, 1975, Anthony Lewis of the *New York Times* wrote a column titled, "Avoiding A Bloodbath," in which he said, "Some will find the whole bloodbath debate unreal. What future possibility could be more terrible than the reality of what is happening in Cambodia now?" How about as many as three million people killed by Pol Pot and his successors? That is nearly one-third of Cambodia's entire population. Does that qualify as "more terrible" than what was happening ten years ago?

Representative Chris Dodd told his House colleagues on March 12, 1975, "The greatest gift our country can give to the Cambodian people is not guns but peace. And the best way to accomplish that goal is by ending military aid now." May the three million rest in peace! Was that the kind of "peace" Mr. Dodd had in mind?

*The New Republic* editorialized on May 3, 1975, "But the excruciating agony suffered by Vietnam and Cambodia is largely of our making."

In the same issue of that visionary publication, Gerald Hickey wrote, "When the guns of the Vietnam War have at last fallen silent, the peace that follows will be a new and in many respects strange experience for a whole generation of Vietnamese." Hickey was right. Death at the hands of Communist butchers is always a new and strange experience for those who have not yet gone through it.

The prediction I liked best, though, came a few years earlier during a speech on the Senate floor by former South Dakota Senator George McGovern. On December 3, 1969, McGovern delivered another of his lengthy monologues opposing U.S. involvement in Vietnam. He quoted a Cornell professor, George T. Kahin, who he described as "among this country's most knowledgeable scholars on Asian affairs." And what did McGovern find so appealing about Professor Kahin? It was the conclusions he drew from the French experience in Indochina which led him to believe there would be no bloodbath in the region if U.S. forces were withdrawn.

Said the professor, ". . . during the entire three-year period following the armistice, they (the International Control Commission) indicate allegations of only 55 incidents of political reprisal (in North Vietnam) . . . During the same period (the Commission) cited allegations involving a total of 1404 incidents of political reprisal in the South involving murder, arrest, confiscation of property and in some cases massacres of several families or whole villages . ."

In fact, McGovern quotes the professor as saying that the ten to fifteen thousand who were eventually killed in the North more than two years after the Geneva armistice died as "a consequence of a clumsy and unrealistic attempt to impose a Chinese communist model of agrarian reorganization . . . As a consequence, these agrarian policies were discredited and dropped and Hanoi's minister of agriculture sacked."

We can all be grateful for that, can't we? Wonder who the minister of agriculture is these days? His program seems to be working a lot better than his predecessor's as he now has enough human fertilizer to last for more than a century.

The Communists may not keep their promises when it comes to arms control agreements, but they are faithful to one overriding principle, echoed by every Soviet leader since Lenin: "All is moral if it advances the cause of Communism."

The pundits and the politicians who predicted no bloodbath after the U.S. withdrawal from Indochina have been proven grossly mistaken. Maybe now, more people will listen to Alexander Solzhenitsyn, who quoted in *The Gulag Archipelago* one of the chief Soviet prosecutors in the post-Bolshevik revolutionary period, N. V. Krylenko: "People are not people, but carriers of specific ideas. No matter what the individual qualities of the defendant, only one method of evaluating him is to be applied: evaluation from the point of view of class expediency."

To paraphrase Peter, Paul, and Mary, when will we ever learn? When will we ever learn? Happy anni-

versary, Vietnam, Cambodia, and Laos. Don't bother
to send cards. Chances are, the intended recipients are
dead.

"HOW DO I KNOW THIS IS A GOOD HONEST BRIBE AND NOT ONE
OF THOSE UNDERHANDED ABSCAM THINGS?"

# The unwritten rule

It is called the unwritten rule. It is a rule that no one imposed. Journalists impose it on themselves. It says that reporters must not disclose the private indiscretions of a public figure unless those indiscretions affect his public life.

The unwritten rule was in force again in the John Fedders case. Fedders, the now former director of law enforcement for the Securities and Exchange Commission, resigned after it became public that he periodically beat his wife during their eighteen-year marriage.

The *Wall Street Journal* sat on the story for more than a year after receiving a tip, unwilling to write about it until the matter became public. The rationale? The *Journal* did not want to wreck the life of a public official. Columnist James J. Kilpatrick defended the unwritten rule and the *Journal's* application of it.

The same scenario has been played out in the past. Former House Ways and Means Committee Chairman Wilbur Mills was known to have had a serious drinking problem, but it was only when he cavorted in a public fountain with a stripper that the press reported it.

Former Ohio Congressman Wayne Hayes was known to be having a sexual encounter with Elizabeth Ray, but it was not until she wound up on the public payroll with no, shall we say "office skills," that the press blew the whistle.

Much was known of the exploits of some male members of the Kennedy family, but nothing was reported because the boys showed up for work on time and kept their hands out of the public till.

More recently, one of the leading critics of South Africa's apartheid system, black clergyman Allan Boesak, was reported to be having an extramarital affair with a white woman. This time, Boesak's Dutch Reformed church and not the press sought to separate private from public morality by exonerating him after he testified that the affair had been a "unique" and innocent one. The church apparently found absolution was warranted because the government press was using the affair to discredit Boesak's political position.

The "unwritten rule" is a lousy one. Leaving aside whether men (and they usually are men) could be persuaded to seek help if they knew reporters might make their private sins public, the larger question begging to be asked is whether we want public officials who lead a Jekyll-Hyde lifestyle.

While watching a recent television program on the environment, narrated by Walter Cronkite, I heard America's most trusted man say this concerning air, water, and land: "I don't think a person can be a leader unless he understands the total interconnectedness of all things." If that applies to the environment, how much more should it apply to the "interconnectedness" between private and public morality?

When riotous living became promotable, there was no longer any need to require good behavior in private as well as in public; no need to require (or expect) any interconnectedness between a person's private behavior and beliefs and his career. Politicians soon accepted this dichotomy, which is in full flower today under the "I'm personally opposed, but . . ." banner. Its extreme application came in the case of Rep. Gerry Studds (D-Mass.) who refused to apologize for having a homosexual encounter with a page and who was reelected by constituents who saw no need for a private moral standard, only a public one.

Having accepted this premise of a split moral personality, it is a very short step to say, "Sure, Stalin was a tyrant, but he made the trains run on time."

The issue goes to the very heart, not only of what a person is, but of what a nation wants from its leadership. I'm not talking about those who drink and occasionally get drunk or go to the track once in a while or periodically have rows with their spouses. All of us have human failings of which we are not proud. Most of us, however, are doing our best to change for the better.

I'm talking about those who get roaring drunk regularly, who are compulsive gamblers, and who beat up on their wives. Are these the types of people we want serving as our leaders in state and national government? In these cases, should private morality be one of the qualifications for public service? And is it only a matter of time before jaded private morality manifests itself as jaded public practice?

The reason I believe most of what has come to be known as the "media elite" tend to subscribe to this unwritten rule is because many of them are guilty (or can see how they might someday be guilty, or know of colleagues who are guilty) of the same behavior. On many occasions I have seen reporters drunk or known of women or men with whom they were sleeping and to whom they were not married. No wonder the only kind of morality they want to recognize is the public kind. No wonder this rule has been unwritten for so long.

# Experts at it again

It was that great Chinese-American philosopher Charlie Chan who remarked, "Expert is merely man who make quick decision and is sometimes right." Charlie's wisdom could be applied to the Alan Guttmacher Institute, the left hand of Planned Parenthood, which has just released a new study indicating that pregnancy rates in Europe are far below those in the United States. The reason, according to the study, is the widespread availability of contraceptives throughout much of Europe.

There is no question that teen pregnancy rates in the United States are incredibly high. According to the Guttmacher Institute, ninety-six out of 1000 teens between the ages of fifteen and nineteen become pregnant every year in the U.S. compared to fourteen per 1000 in the Netherlands, thirty-five in Sweden, forty-three in France, and forty-five in England and Wales.

But is the solution, as the Guttmacher study contends, more readily available contraceptives and more intense sex education in America? I don't think so.

The Guttmacher-Planned Parenthood approach to sex measures success by how well it prevents unwanted pregnancy and venereal disease. It is less concerned, protestations to the contrary, with the moral and social development of a child.

That is why sex education guru Mary Calderone says of a book written by a colleague, "It is immensely refreshing in its openness, candor, realism—and particularly in its lack of authoritarianism, moralism, and dogmatism." These last three are code words, of course, for values derived from religious faith. In this view, a dose of God is more hazardous to one's psyche than a dose of herpes.

This philosophy says that it may be OK to control a child's access to candy, liquor, and the family car, but by golly we had better make sure he knows about intercourse in kindergarten, whether he is ready for it or not.

The Guttmacher report omits as much as it reports. For example, it omits findings published by the Denmark government. Those findings show that since compulsory sex education was adopted in Denmark in 1970 and all pornography, abortion, homosexuality, and incest involving those eighteen and over became legal, there has, indeed, been a drop in the birth rate, but the price has been high. Illegitimate births, which were supposed to drop, instead nearly doubled; abortion rates,

which were predicted to fall with the ready availability of condoms and other contraceptives in grocery stores, actually doubled; venereal disease more than doubled, and divorces doubled. The only categories showing decreases were sex crimes (that was because nearly all of them, except rape, which went up, were decriminalized) and the age of first intercourse.

Sweden is the most "sexually liberated" country in the world. Swedish parents are forbidden by law to spank their children. Yet, the suicide rate among Sweden's teenagers is the highest in the world. And Amsterdam has the dubious distinction of being the world's child pornography capital.

According to the Senate Subcommittee on the Family, while there may have been a reduction in the number of teenagers having babies, there has been a marked increase in teen abortions.

With more than 5,000 "family planning clinics" now operating in the U.S., many of them with the help of federal funds, and sex education courses in many public schools, it is clear that contraceptive information alone is not the solution to the unwanted consequences of sexual activity.

Dr. Jacqueline Kasun of Humboldt State University in San Francisco says there was a drop in adolescent pregnancies before Planned Parenthood programs began moving into California in the 1960s. Now, she says, "after years of extremely high expenditures and effort in this area, we have the highest rate of teen pregnancy in the entire nation . . . and the highest rate of teen abortion."

One does not teach a teenager to drive a car by saying, "Here, kid. Take the keys and learn the rules of the road for yourself." One cannot successfully teach a child about sex outside of "moral rules of the road." In each instance, unwanted consequences are likely to occur.

My suspicion is that parents have grown tired of these so-called "experts" telling them how to rear their children and would appreciate the state looking after parental interests once in a while. After all, what should the goal of a nation's school system be: to produce a well-rounded and socially responsible young adult, or to create a morally neutral robot who never has to think about the consequences of his or her actions.

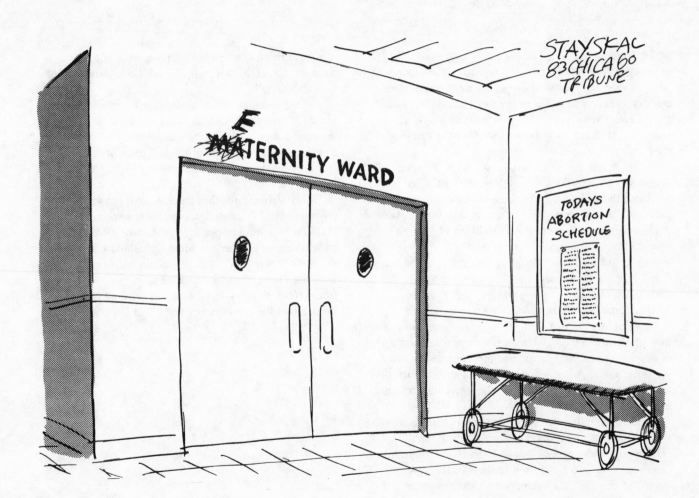

# Whistle blower

If Sandy Tosti had been employed by the Pentagon as a cost overrun specialist and not by Plantation General Hospital as a nurse, if she had been dismissed because she blew the whistle on excessive military spending and not because she protested the destruction of a twenty-two-week-old baby who survived a botched abortion, maybe she would be featured on the cover of a national magazine. Instead, she is being ignored.

Sandy Tosti alleges that she was dismissed from her job in the neonatology unit of the hospital because she called a friend and asked her to pray for the baby that it might survive. The friend called another friend, and that friend called a local newspaper. The newspaper called the hospital.

The hospital contends that Sandy caused it to receive "bad publicity," but Sandy says she was merely exercising her First Amendment rights of free religious expression. She says she would have done the same for a cancer patient.

Sandy has retained attorney Tom Bush, a former member of the Florida legislature. She has filed a damage suit in excess of $100,000, charging the hospital with a violation of equal employment opportunity laws.

The allegations in the suit are these: On February 19, an abortion was performed by a physician on a woman who was twenty-two weeks or more pregnant at Plantation General Hospital. The prostiglandin suppository method was used, a method which produces strong contractions that are supposed to suffocate the baby and result in a stillbirth. The baby survived the abortion and was later discovered by the staff in the neonatal unit, which assumed it was a normal premature birth.

The suit contends that standard care usually given to newborns was provided to the baby girl until a phone call was received by the neonatologist from another physician, who allegedly indicated he had been told to unplug the baby's life support system due to the fact that the baby was the result of an abortion.

Attorney Bush says that Florida law requires all babies to be treated the same, whether they are the result of an abortion or a premature birth. Someone apparently forgot to tell the doctor.

According to the suit, while the neonatal staff did not "pull the plug," care for the baby shifted from "life saving treatment" to "conditional care" (care for the dying). The suit contends the shift in care was the result of the phone call from the abortion doctor.

After Sandy phoned a friend to ask that she pray for the baby to survive, the suit alleges that it became "common knowledge" in the neonatal unit that there was a decision to "let the baby go." The suit says certain hospital staff members hoped the baby would die by midnight so that she would not show up on the hospital census for that day, further complicating matters. She died at 1 A.M.

When phone calls began coming into the hospital, Sandy was interrogated by her superiors. It was then, the suit alleges, that she was charged with causing the hospital to receive "bad publicity" and "breaking confidences." The director of nurses, the suit contends, told Sandy that if she did not resign she would be terminated. She refused and was fired.

Right-to-life groups have called for an investigation into the matter. The State Attorney's office has been asked to conduct a probe, but so far no official action has been taken. The hospital claims efforts to save the baby were "heroic."

Sandy says the "putting aside" of babies (the euphemism that is used in place of "letting them die") occurs frequently at Plantation General and at other hospitals around the country. She says some babies are covered with a blanket and allowed to "gasp their lives away." Sometimes, she says, when this method is too slow, a doctor will kill the baby manually by withdrawing blood from the newborn's heart with a syringe.

Not very pleasant to contemplate, is it? No wonder this is considered "bad publicity." Now you know why photographers were not welcome at Auschwitz.

Sandy says the tragedy was compounded because there was another prematurely born baby in the neonatal unit that night. That baby was the same age as the one chosen for death, about twenty-two weeks. Today that baby is healthy and growing and headed for a normal life, because someone determined it had a right to live. But the baby who survived the abortion had the misfortune to be declared unfit to live twice and her life was destroyed.

Though a "heroine" to some, Sandy no doubt will be known as a "troublemaker" or "religious fanatic" at Plantation General. A local Catholic hospital, which does not perform abortions, hired her, but that is little consolation for what she has been through.

Florida law says that no employee, physician, nurse, or hospital can be required to participate in an abortion and that no hospital may threaten someone with dismissal because they object to or refuse to participate in an abortion. It will be interesting to see how this case comes out. It is too bad that the outcome will not bring back the baby girl who was killed.

# Morality and nuclear weapons

The question before the house in the world's "most famous debating union," as they somewhat pretentiously like to say here, was preposterous on its face: "All nuclear weapons are morally indefensible." One could easily respond by proclaiming the slogan of the National Rifle Association that "guns don't kill people; people kill people," but they expect more from you at Oxford.

The debate between students on both sides of the question preceded in prize-fight fashion the "main event" between the suddenly recognizable Prime Minister of New Zealand, David Lange, and Reverend Jerry Falwell of the Moral Majority.

As one watched and listened to the debate, which was televised live in New Zealand and Australia, one had to be struck by a compelling truth; namely, that when Westerners contend about such matters, they speak to a limited audience, reaching only those who share their own moral presuppositions. These presuppositions would include the basic value and dignity of man before God, and our accountability to our fellowmen, to the state, and ultimately to God for our actions. A commitment to freedom and personal liberty for the individual flows from these basic premises. Regardless of how those of us in what used to be called the "free world" may disagree on political matters, this philosophy is, and always has been, at the heart of Western democratic principles.

Therefore, as Prime Minister Lange observed that "Europe and the United States are ringed with nuclear weapons, and their people have never been more at risk," his words seemed persuasive only to those in the packed hall who shared his Western values. Even his assertion that "there are some things worse than living under Communism," which he said includes starvation in Ethiopia (better Red than not fed?), found willing acceptance among the naive in the hall who had so recently stuffed themselves at dinner and who planned to sleep peaceably in their own beds later that night.

Forty-four years earlier, Franklin Roosevelt declared at Oxford that "We, too, born to freedom, and believing in freedom, are willing to fight to maintain freedom. We, and all others who believe as deeply as we do, would rather die on our feet than live on our knees."

Now comes David Lange asserting the old "bet-

Dear English Protester: How would you like your missiles delivered?
the american way...
U.S.
or the Russian way?
Sincerely, Wayne Stayskal
83 CHICAGO TRIBUNE

ter Red than dead'' view to which Solzhenitsyn has offered the ultimate rejoinder: "To be Red is to be dead, but more slowly."

Lange tried to have it both ways. He rejected the American nuclear umbrella, but when challenged to pull out of the ANZUS pact to demonstrate his consistency, he refused, saying, "I prefer to change it from within." It is like living at home with parents until one is fifty years old, all the while refusing to do any chores. One enjoys all of the benefits, but bears few of the responsibilities.

The problem with debates like these is that the Marxist philosophy against which the West has defended itself is marching to a far different drummer and is, indeed, in another parade altogether.

Every Soviet leader since Lenin has said that "all is moral if it advances the cause of Communism." In fact, Lenin wrote, before he came to power, that one of the reasons for the failure of early attempts at revolution in eighteenth-century France was that they didn't kill enough people.

As the late philosopher-theologian Dr. Francis Schaeffer observed, "The Europeans who are leaders in government have understood the reality of what Winston Churchill said immediately after World War Two—that with their overwhelming forces the Soviets could easily dominate Western Europe if it were not for the deterrent of U.S. atomic weapons."

Regrettable and costly as they may be, had the West not possessed nuclear weapons and been perceived as willing to use them as a last resort (thereby insuring the unlikelihood of their ever having to be used), could there be any serious doubt that all of Western Europe, including England itself, would by now have fallen under the hammer and sickle? Those who believe otherwise must have looked upon good old Joe Stalin as a nice fellow.

That the resolution on the immorality of nuclear weapons was upheld by a 298-250 margin is encouraging when one considers the leftward ideology of many of the students.

But the most telling point of the evening came when a small group of "peace demonstrators" unfurled a banner from the balcony and began shouting slogans. The last time I saw that happen was when evangelist Billy Graham spoke at a church in Moscow. Then, the demonstrators were arrested and hauled away, never to be heard from again. At Oxford, though, the demonstrators had their say and left without any confrontation with the police. In fact, there were no police around at all. This one incident dramatically emphasized, even more than the debate, why such a system is worth defending, even with nuclear weapons, and why no price is too high when the alternative is slavery.

# The government is my keeper

Thirty-six religious leaders must have been having a slow day when they all got together in New York and issued a statement which said, "Poverty in this country can and must end. Out of our faith grows the conviction that no one, child or adult, should suffer the debilitation of poverty."

Did the religious leaders announce a new offensive by churches and synagogues to help end the poverty? Of course not. They called on government to do it.

It is always easy to be compassionate with someone else's time and money. But show me a Torah, a Koran, or an Epistle that says, "the government is my keeper, I shall not want; the government maketh me to lie down in green pastures; the government restoreth my soul; yeah, though I walk through the valley of the shadow of death, the Department of Health and Human Services is with me; my food stamps and welfare checks, they comfort me." That was the catechism of The Great Society, whose "deity," Lyndon Baines Johnson, nearly spent the whole nation into bankruptcy, but failed to end poverty.

Those who would resuscitate the Great Society are looking in the wrong place. As Senator Dan Quayle (R-Ind.) told the *Wall Street Journal,* "You have to believe people realize there's going to be less federal money to pass around. We've got to get people conditioned to that idea." The religious leaders in New York apparently are not yet in condition.

President Reagan correctly summarized the best way to sharply reduce poverty in America during an opening statement at his February 22 news conference: "America has rediscovered that the key to greater economic growth, opportunity, prosperity for all is to unharness the energies of free enterprise. The American miracle of which the world now speaks is a triumph of free people and their private institutions, not government. It was individual workers, business people, entrepreneurs—not government—who created virtually every one of our seven million new jobs over the past two years."

The President is trying to reintroduce Americans to what made this country strong and great in the first place. Emerson summarized it in his essay on "Self-Reliance."

Said Ralph Waldo, "There is a time in every man's

education when he arrives at the conviction that envy is ignorance; that imitation is suicide; that he must take himself for better for worse as his portion; that though the wide universe is full of good, no kernal of nourishing corn can come to him but through his toil bestowed on that plot of ground which is given to him to till. The power that resides in him is new in nature, and none but he knows what that is which he can do, nor does he know until he has tried."

The puzzle today is that so many do not want to try. It is easier to accept a government check than to accept the obligation and drudgery of looking for work. What if welfare were ended tomorrow except for the handicapped and others unable to work at all? Would famine grip the nation? Would American streets resemble the sands of Ethiopia? Hardly.

The problem, as the President has pointed out, is that government continues to spend more than it takes in. Those of us who have occasionally abused our credit cards know what happens in our personal affairs. The only difference is that the government can print its money. We have to get ours the old-fashioned way by earning it.

Going back to the bankrupt days of The Great Society in an attempt to end poverty means repeating the mistakes of the past.

The religious leaders would have done well to consider the immortal words of one Harry F. Banks, who said, "A good place to find a helping hand is at the end of your arm," instead of trying again to use their hands to pick the pocket of Uncle Sam.

# The politics of selfishnesss

The other day on the House floor, Rep. Patricia Schroeder (D-Colo.) coined one of those phrases that look great in headlines.

The debate was over the nearly bankrupt Social Security system and over which politicians are the least sensitive to the elderly. Between slams at the President for his alleged indifference to the elderly, Mrs. Schroeder took a shot at her state's governor, Richard Lamm, for his now infamous remark that the old and terminally ill "have got a duty to die and to get out of the way."

Said Mrs. Schroeder, "So let us all work to-gether...lower all of that rhetoric, stop the politics of selfishness...you can play the politics of selfishness on young people. But that is wrong, and we must stop it...That generation (seniors) did not play the politics of selfishness and they do not deserve to be treated this way and we are not going to stand for that in this day and age."

The tragedy now being played out against the elderly stems from the unwillingness of political leaders to understand that the "politics of selfishness" was created out of a callous disregard for the value of human life. When a "quality of life" ethic replaces a "sanctity of life" ethic, the politics of selfishness is the inevitable result.

Curiously, Mrs. Schroeder invokes a word and concept that one does not hear used much these days. It it the word "wrong." She said it is wrong to engage in the politics of selfishness; wrong to treat older people the way they are now being treated; wrong to tell them that they have a duty to die and get out of the way. But why is it wrong? She doesn't say, presumably leaving the question for philosophers to ponder.

One does not have to subscribe to the domino theory in international relations to understand how it works in the area of human relations.

The abortion domino fell in 1973. The infanticide domino, the killing of Baby Does, fell close behind, and now the euthanasia domino is teetering as well. It would seem we have adopted an ethic that allows the extermination of the unborn because they are not fully human and the termination of the newly born because they are too great an economic and emotional drain. If that is so, then what moral claim can an elderly person make when Gov. Lamm or one of his agents proclaims that

"I KNEW I SHOULD HAVE ABORTED YOU LIKE ALL THE REST, LEON!"

the lives of the elderly are no longer worth living; that they should die quickly so their humus may enrich the soil that nourishes the young?

Mr. Lamm may not be Boris Karloff, but he certainly is Igor, the mad scientist's assistant. The Frankenstein's monster they have spawned is about to gobble up its creators, who have no power to stop what they have unleashed.

In 1977, the Philadelphia *Bulletin* carried an Associated Press story which reported that a British doctor, John Goundry, predicted a "death pill" will be available and perhaps obligatory by the end of the century. The story said doctors should be able to give such a pill to old people if they ask for it. Mr. Goundry also said, "In the end I can see the state taking over and insisting on euthanasia." He is not alone.

*The Seattle Times* reported last month that Seattle's University Hospital is now allowing women to abort babies of the "wrong" sex. If amniocentesis reveals that a woman is carrying a girl and she wants a boy, or the reverse, the hospital will help her abort the child.

Before the abortion domino fell, we were told that abortion-on-demand was necessary to relieve the suffering of thirteen-year-old girls who had been raped. Now sex selection is part of the equation. So is infanticide. Is this but a preview of coming attractions?

What is the basis for human dignity, for human life? If it is not Jefferson's maxim that "all men are created equal and are endowed by our Creator with certain inalienable rights" and that among them is the inalienable right to live, then we are participants in the politics of selfishness, no matter how such politics might be deplored by those who helped to inaugurate them.

# Evil does exist, and it describes Soviets' "empire"

Last year, before the pragmatists at the White House had finished lobotomizing the President, and Reagan, on occasion, could still be Reagan, the President delivered a tough speech to the National Association of Evangelicals in Orlando, in which he accused the Soviet Union of being an "evil empire" and the focus of evil in the world.

Those who felt that the real focus of evil was the President and his supposed insensitivity to the poor were outraged. Some even questioned whether the concept of evil was a fit subject for discussion in international affairs in this "enlightened age."

What the President said and the overreaction to his remarks came back to me when I read two comments on the subject of evil, printed in the *New York Times*. One was a quotation by Vice President George Bush, at a groundbreaking ceremony for the U.S. Holocaust Memorial Museum in Washington: "The Holocaust stands testament to man's moral imperfections. In every one of us is interwoven *evil* with goodness, impulse with restraint, cruelty with gentleness."

Just below, in a coincidental juxtaposition, was a paid ad from Gus Hall, the Communist Party candidate for President. Hall said, "The bloody military takeover of Grenada stands as a stark reminder of the *evil* intentions of U.S policy in Central America."

Two perceptions of evil

I don't know what the Soviet dictionary says of evil, but Webster's offers several options: "(1) morally reprehensible; sinful; wicked; arising from actual or imputed bad character or conduct; (2) something that brings sorrow, distress or calamity; (3) the fact of suffering, misfortune and wrongdoing."

Perhaps Gus Hall would say that all of those definitions fit the United States, but the fact is that for sixty-seven years, Soviet communism, domestic and exported, and for thirty-four years Chinese communism, has been responsible for the deaths of an estimated 147 million people. For 208 years, American democracy, domestically and abroad, has for the most part been a liberating experience which has fueled humankind's highest aspirations. If it were not so, why must we institute immigration quotas and build fences to keep people out, while our adversaries must employ walls, fences, and armed guards to keep people in?

Interview people, conduct a Gallup Poll in

Communist paradises, and if those polled are honest, America will receive most-favored-nation status.

Some writers, social commentators, even theologians, would have us believe that evil does not exist. But history proves otherwise.

Was Hitler evil or just in need of a B. F. Skinner behavior modification course? What about Idi Amin? And these are only two recent incarnations of evil. History is full of others.

Edmund Burke said at the founding of our nation that "All that is necessary for evil to triumph is for good men to do nothing."

The Vice President was right when he said that evil coexists with good in every one of us. But in America, the good is the standard by which men's hearts and motives are measured, thereby insuring that the good will not be "interred with their bones."

In the Communist system, the devaluation of human beings to little more than slaves of the state insures that good is subordinated to the evil desires of leadership. Such a policy guarantees a quicker internment for those who attempt to impose good on the system.

Alexander Solzhenitsyn was right when he said that it is not a question of being Red or dead. "To be Red," he observed, "is to be dead, but more slowly."

Evil must and can be overcome; with good where possible and with force where necessary. Goodness will not overcome force, but force can overcome goodness.

That is a lesson we have not yet learned in Central America or anywhere else where our vital interests are now being threatened.

# Health hazards

What can be more hazardous to the health and welfare of public school students: exposure to venereal disease or exposure to the possiblity of the existence of God?

The other day I received a letter from the mother of a thirteen-year-old girl in Virgina. Her daughter attends an eighth grade class at a public school.

The woman is concerned because the school recently presented a three-day study of venereal disease. She is not opposed to the study. What upsets her is the way it is taught.

Says she, "Some of the things that concern me are that the classes are mixed. Another thing that bothered me is that the parents weren't notified. I called two other mothers to see how they felt about it, and they didn't even know that the classes had been done! From what my daughter told me, the film that was shown gave the impression that getting VD is nothing to be ashamed of —it's just a disease and even good people get it. A toll-free number was given for students to call and receive treatment without their parents ever having to know about it!

"The teacher conducting the class asked the girls the following question: 'If your boyfriend found out he had VD, would you want him to tell you himself, or would you want him to get people from the clinic to call and tell you that he had VD?' To me this kind of questioning is implying that all children in this age group are sexually active."

The letter arrived in between the Senate's rejection of a voluntary school prayer amendment and the defeat in the House of the Equal Access Bill.

What, then, are we left to conclude? The message that comes through loud and clear is that a dose of God is to be considered more hazardous to the health of public school children than a dose of herpes.

The schools are prohibited from handing out the equivalent of God's toll-free number, but they feel mandated to show films that depict all eighth graders as sexually active and provide information designed to undermine parental authority and responsibility for their minor children.

What would be wrong with teaching children about the greatest contraceptive and prophylaxis ever developed: the word "No"? What about alternatives to sex such as chastity and self-control and remaining faithful, once married, to one partner for life? Not only are such alternatives guaranteed to prevent venereal disease; they also go a long way toward alleviating the psychological, emotional and spiritual damage that too often follows early sexual experimentation.

If the critics of voluntary prayer are right (and I do not believe they are) that such a procedure would result in the forcing of one faith or belief or practice on some who do not hold similar views, then what, pray tell, is being forced on children who must watch films with toll-free numbers to their friendly neighborhood VD clinic?

Children who cannot attend certain movies without being accompanied by an adult, who cannot have their ears pierced without a note from home, who are forbidden to receive as much as an aspirin from the school nurse without parental consent in writing, are told that if they reach out and touch someone sexually and get VD, they can reach out and touch, courtesy of A T & T, and "dial a clinic," parental guidance not suggested.

The times and our entire thought processes are out of joint.

Who produces these films? Do the producers have a perspective they are trying to advance? Are they connected with the Planned Parenthood circle that is much involved in the one-dimensional sex education courses taught in our public schools? I say one-dimensional be-cause such courses rarely, if ever, discuss or promote self-control as the best option. Why should they? It is in their interest to keep the sex machine well oiled.

Just as florists hate the phrase, "in lieu of flowers..." so, too, do the merchants of sex break out in hives when anyone suggests, "in lieu of sex..."

"YOU MAY WRITE A REPORT ON ANY INSECT YOU'D LIKE ... EXCEPT, OF COURSE, THE PRAYING MANTIS!"

STAYSKAL
82 CHICAGO
TRIBUNE

"TELL ME... DO YOU BELIEVE IN LIFE AFTER NUCLEAR WAR?"

# The revolutionary uses of religion

The American military operation in Grenada last October produced not only the short-term benefit of freeing the tiny Caribbean island from Cuban domination, but also uncovered thousands of pounds of documents which have proved to be the equivalent of discovering the other team's playbook on the eve of the Super Bowl.

Among the documents which analysts in Washington are still sifting through is a top-secret memo dated July 12, 1983, from a Major Keith Roberts, chief of internal security for the New Jewel Movement. The NJM had consummated a secret agreement with the Cuban Communist Party to conduct a sort of Peace Corps in reverse.

The Roberts memo details a sophisticated plan for subverting the churches in Grenada and eventually turning them into tools of the revolution. The first step in that process was already under way, with Grenadians being sent to Cuba for training in church subversion and infiltration and Cubans coming to Grenada to begin the work while their buddies were in class.

The campaign was carried out in a variety of ways. Given a pretext, the government would simply get rid of religious leaders who were explicitly anti-Communist. The internal subversion of the church would be more detailed, but just as effective.

The Roberts memo called for "removal from primary schools, all deeply religious head teachers by whatever means most suitable, replacing them with more progressive elements; the introduction of political education in every classroom in the primary and secondary schools; political education for all teachers; cut back on all religous programs on Radio Free Grenada, substituting on Sunday morning voice cast of the masses on the progress of the projects; to promote contacts among clergymen and members of laity from Nicaragua and other Latin American countries linked to the theology of liberation and, in general, the church commitment to revolutionary positions; opening Marxist-Leninist bookshops in different parishes of the country; getting Marxist-Leninist literature into all schools; step up the systematic monitoring of all religious manifestation in the state, and position being taken as regards the work permit of way-side preachers entering the country to preach, and immigration position on these way-side preachers; open cinemas; start progressive churches (talk with Nicaraguans and Cubans)."

In commenting on the document, The Institute on Religion and Democracy in Washington, D.C., which monitors religious persecution in Communist countries, noted that immediately after the U.S. invasion, something in this country called "The Committee in Solidarity with Free Grenada" issued a press release under the headline, "Religious and Community Leaders Condemm U.S. Invasion of Grenada."

The release came from a staff person at the Latin American Affairs office of the United Methodist Church at the United Nations. Among the signers of the release were a number of officials of the U.S. National Council of Churches.

As I recall, the NCC moved heaven and earth in an attempt to convince folks that a CBS "60 Minutes" report and a *Readers Digest* story were inaccurate when they asserted that the church body underwrote Third World revolutions.

The discovery of the Grenada documents has served another useful purpose besides that of outflanking the Cubans in Grenada and discovering their game plan for all of Latin America.

It has shown us what liberal churches in America mean by the "doctrine of separation of church and state." It bears a striking resemblance to what the Cubans mean when they try to separate church *from* state.

# Pornography and first amendment freedoms

The Reagan Administration's pledge to crack down on pornography, particularly child pornography, and recent hearings in Washington by the Senate Juvenile Justice Subcommittee are again going to raise questions we have heard before; questions about individual liberty and the rights of other individuals to be free from the consequences of porn.

For years we have heard the argument from those who would consider themselves First Amendment purists that once something makes its way onto the printed page it is holy writ, never to be tampered with by man or beast, even when men become beasts while digesting some of the material. That argument may not hold as much water as it once did because evidence is piling up that a steady diet of pornography may, like cigarettes, cause serious problems.

Children as young as nine testified before the Senate subcommittee that they had been sexually abused by baby-sitters, family "friends," and acquaintances. Recently we have heard other stories of child molestation, including Senator Paula Hawkins' (R-Fla.) touching revelation that she had been molested at the age of five.

The National Association of Social Workers estimates that one in eight American females will be the victim of sexual abuse before the age of eighteen. Incidents of sexual abuse against young boys by men is increasing rapidly.

What do these figures have to do with pornography? Plenty!

The last time a Presidential commission looked into the subject was 1970, when a majority of the commission found there was not enough evidence to link pornography with sex crimes. But a minority demurred. Father Morton A. Hill, who now heads Morality in Media in New York, and Dr. Winfrey C. Link issued a minority report which included statistics that strongly suggested a connection between pornography and sexual abuse.

One study authorized by the Commission included interviews with convicted sex criminals. It found that 55 percent of the rapists reported being excited to sex relations by pornography. When reporting on peak experiences in exposure to pornography during their teens, 80 percent of the rapists reported wishing to try the act that they had witnessed or seen demonstrated

"AND FURTHERMORE, WE DEMAND THAT EACH VIEWING DAY BE STARTED WITH A MOMENT OF SILENT PORNOGRAPHY!"

in the pornography. When asked whether they did follow through with such sexual activity immediately or shortly thereafter, 30 percent of the rapists replied, "Yes."

In another study, it was found that "254 psychiatrists and psychologists had cases where they reported they had seen/found a direct causal linkage betwen involvement with pornography and a sex crime. Another 324 professionals reported seeing cases where such a relationship was suspected."

Responding to critics who say obscenity and pornography laws are an attempt to legislate individual morality and freedom of choice, Hill-Link said, "Obscenity law in no way legislates individual morality, but provides protection for public morality."

Fourteen years after the last Presidential Commission studied pornography and obscenity, perverted and illicit sex has proliferated in movies, magazines, on television, and in the record industry. Paralleling that proliferation has been a skyrocketing of sex crimes of all types, particularly against children.

The Preamble to the Constitution speaks of promoting the "general welfare." Can any reasonable case be made that pornography, which excites some people to sexually abuse children, promotes the general welfare? If ever there was a case where the government ought to be looking out for the rights of victims ahead of the rights of "sickos," this is the case. It is to be hoped that the newest Presidential Commission will find a majority in agreement that something needs to be done and needs to be done now!

"SHE HAD NO RIGHT ABORTING ME ... AFTER ALL, IT'S MY BODY!"

# Newspeak, newthink

Talk about raw judicial power!

The California Court of Appeals ruled that 16,000 fetuses preserved in formaldehyde since their discovery inside a repossessed container two years ago may not be given human burial rights because they are not human. The court did not say that these fetuses were not persons, which would have aligned it with the language chosen by the Supreme Court in 1973 in the *Roe vs. Wade* case. It said the fetuses were not human.

In using such language, the California court has at once denied fetoscopy, embryology, studies in fetal pain, and the naked eye. If these unfortunate nonpersons are not human, what are they? Giraffes? Automobiles?

One cannot critique the court's "logic" because none was evident in the ruling. Presiding Justice Arleigh Woods, citing the presence of the Catholic League for Religious and Civil Rights as an intervenor in the case said, "It is clear from the record that the Catholic League is a religious organization which regards a fetus as a human being and abortion as murder. While this specific belief may cross sectarian lines, it is a belief not universally held. Consequently, any state action showing a preference for this belief will be strictly scrutinized and must be invalidated unless it is justified by compelling government interest." The mind boggles at this latest demonstration of Orwellian "Newspeak" and "Newthink."

Both the *Dred Scott* decision in 1857 which upheld slavery, and the *Roe vs. Wade* decision in 1973, which allows abortion-on-demand, saw the Supreme Court classify certain categories of people as noncitizens, nonpersons, or property which could be disposed of at the whim of the "owner." In each case the ruling was made against the tide of public opinion. Both slavery and abortion were at the time of the rulings (and still are now) regarded as immoral by millions of Americans. For Justice Woods to state that these fetuses are not human because some people don't believe they are is ludicrous. Some bigots believe that blacks are subhuman. Would Justice Woods repeal civil rights laws because of such a disagreement? Would he throw out the Equal Rights Amendment if it were ever passed and ratified because a substantial number of persons are opposed to it?

Justice Woods said that since there is no compelling state interest in disposing of the fetuses in a private cemetery, "we perceive the intended burial will enlist the prestige and power of the state. This is Constitutionally forbidden." And what will the order to incinerate the fetuses enlist if not the prestige and power of the state to impose just the opposite view?

A statement issued by Carol Downer of the euphemistically named "Los Angeles Feminist Women's Health Clinic" (read, abortion mill) revealed the antireligious bias in this case: "I'm very relieved that the courts are seeing this in the way they do, which is that it's entirely inappropriate for the religious forces to enter into this situation."

There you have it. Human babies are not really babies because some Catholics (and non-Catholics) think they are, and religious people have no right to participate in a legal proceeding if their faith colors their judgment. Has anyone noticed a spinning motion in the graves of the Founding Fathers?

This case will, no doubt, go to the Supreme Court. In the meantime, the illogic of the California Court of Appeals ruling needs to be examined more closely. In one ruling, the California court moved from a determination that unborn babies are not only nonpersons, but nonhumans and that religious people should not be granted the same political freedoms enjoyed by Madalyn Murray O'Hair. Anyone for a chorus of "We shall overcome someday"?

# Black employees need good self-image

The first thing to be said about the thirty-five page Urban League report on the American black male is that it contains a lot of truth. There *is* a "steady attrition" in the number of black men capable of supporting a wife and children.

The second thing to be said about the report is, what are we going to do about it? More programs alone are not the answer. They do not contribute to a positive self-image, which is the root of the problem.

The Urban League report says the black male is damaged by discrimination that shows up "in the form of self-destructive behavior such as drug abuse and alcoholism that black men are particularly heir to."

Dr. E. V. Hill believes he has found the answer. Hill is pastor of the Mt. Zion Missionary Baptist Church in the Watts area of Los Angeles. He was instrumental in restoring peace to Watts when blacks rioted in 1968. He also served on the President's Commission on Private Sector Initiatives.

Hill says the problem for American black males can be traced to the period immediately following World War II. The black man found it almost impossible to find a job. The federal government instituted a number of what Hill calls "in the meantime programs" to overcome the job disparity faced by black men in the post-war period. Hill sees a need for similar "in the meantime programs" to bridge the job gap for black men today as the country moves into the technological age while waiting for the Reagan administration's economic philosophy, which he supports, to work. He believes the administration was premature in cutting off some of these "in the meantime programs" such as Opportunities Industrialization Center (OIC), which also received foundation and industry support. OIC recruited all unemployed people, even if they were drunkards. They were put through motivational and attitude adjustment courses to qualify them for entry level jobs in industry and were followed up for one year. Eighty percent of them were black men.

In the first six months of the program's operation in Los Angeles, Hill put 743 people into full-time jobs. More than 600 were in day or night classes, and 1,700 were on a waiting list. Hill is fighting to resurrect OIC. He says it is not enough to ask the unemployed to fill out job applications. Many cannot even get through this first step without attitude changes and proper motivation.

"I HOPE I GET ONE OF THOSE JOBS. IT'LL BE NICE TO GET BACK TO WORK AND DEMAND MORE PAY AGAIN!!"

It is here, however, that Hill parts company with those blacks who see programs alone as the answer. Hill, who has had his life threatened by both the Ku Klux Klan and the Black Panther Party, believes that the way black men view themselves is all important. He has proved his solution in the laboratory of life.

Hill tells the following story: "At our church, we had a class just graduate in bus driving. We took twelve unemployed school dropouts. Four were convicted felons. They came in with curlers in their hair and marijuana sticks in their mouths. We kept them for six months. We spent several weeks exposing them to lectures from successful people who used to be where they were. Out of the twelve, six stayed with the program. I took them to a company where I tried to persuade the boss to give these men on-the-job training. He liked them so much they were hired outright and are being paid between ten and twelve dollars an hour. The six dropouts are on the corner, bad-mouthing the President."

Hill is Henry Higgins, and the unemployed are Eliza Doolittle. One of his graduates was a prostitute who now works as an administrative secretary for a television show. "All she needed was a good self-image," he says.

"If the Republican Party," says Hill, "would add just one dimension to its vision, it would have perfect vision. It must prepare the unemployed to enter these new jobs as they come available. The unemployed must be cleaned up on the outside as well as on the inside and then they will enter these jobs with roughly the same equal start enjoyed by others who have not experienced what these mostly black men have gone through."

The Urban League should listen to this. So should the administration.

CHURCH OF WATTS

JESUS SAID,
"COME UNTO ME, ALL
YE THAT LABOUR AND
ARE HEAVY LADEN,
AND I WILL GIVE
YOU REST."

STAYSKAL
84 TAMPA
TRIBUNE

"COULD HAVE FOOLED ME ... I THOUGHT MONDALE SAID THAT
JUST LAST WEEK!"

# Religion at the polls

A new religion has been established in America. It has not been unconstitutionally established by Congress. It is not the religion of secular humanism, as some claim. Neither is it the religion of fundamental Christianity, as others assert.

It is, in the words of Oxford scholar Os Guinness, "privatized religion." The catechism of this new religion was accurately summed up by Dorothy Palumbo, a fifty-eight-year-old home economics teacher at Bishop Carney High School in Brooklyn, who said, "Your faith should not follow you into the voting booth."

The late chairman of McDonald's Corp., Ray Kroc, is reported to have been asked on one of the talk programs about his priorities in life. Mr. Kroc responded, "It's God first, family second, and hamburgers third. But when I get to the office, I reverse the order." Though Mr. Kroc may have said it only to get a laugh, that is precisely the way many people, including Dorothy Palumbo of Brooklyn, Gov. Mario Cuomo of New York, and Vice Presidential nominee Geraldine Ferraro, feel about religious faith.

Can this kind of privatized religion be practical? Is it really religion, or is it a form of pandering to the nonreligious and marginally religious? In other words, can people who really believe in this type of religion practice what they preach, so to speak?

Theologian R. C. Sproul of the Ligonier Valley Study Center in Stahlstown, Pennsylvania, does not think so. Mr. Sproul says that the modern concept of church-state separation, as distinct from what the founding fathers conceived, is, in reality, an attempt to separate God from state. It is like saying that when I enter the voting booth I will remove my head from my body and hand it to the person who pulls the curtain.

Says Mr. Sproul, "The religion that we practice is a religion consigned to a reservation. On the surface it seems like we are dealing with a benign pluralism, but as soon as the Christian steps off the reservation and asserts the Kingship of Christ over all of creation, then we find that the benign secularist starts to snarl."

Mr. Sproul would say to those like Dorothy Palumbo, Mr. Cuomo, and Mrs. Ferraro, "The idea of a God who only reigns over the church is basically practical atheism, because a God who is only sovereign over the church is no God at all."

Mr. Sproul is concerned not only about religious illiteracy, but by a lack of understanding in the electorate of what it means to vote. The Latin root for vote is *votum,* which means "desire."

Americans believe that voting is a form of expressing our desires. When enough of us, a majority, express our desires, we prevail over those who are expressing their desires, including desires that are antithetical to those of the majority. Those in the majority, under our form of government, may then enforce their desires upon the rest of the nation. This, of course, is a form of coercion, but it is coercion in what we believe to be a positive sense, unlike the coercion of a totalitarian state.

The expression of desires in this way, Mr. Sproul believes, is at odds with biblical teaching. He believes that righteousness and justice are the only principles for which a Christian has an obligation to vote. By obligation he means that if justice demands that the government should act, as in civil rights for blacks, then policies and people who support civil rights should receive our votes.

But, he says, if I am a woman and my desire is to rid myself of unborn human life because it is not convenient for me to carry that life, then justice and righteousness demand that I be prohibited from doing so. When politicians claim that every woman has a right to her own body and a right to an abortion, we must ask, "Where does that right come from? Who gave you that right?" If the right comes only from the state, then there is nothing wrong with using power politics to reverse the decision of the state (and let's allow the bigots to overturn open housing laws while we're at it, too).

Mr. Sproul believes the moral crisis we now face, which has led to the "I'm personally opposed, but . . ." silliness, has arrived because of our inability to distinguish between rights and desires. Nineteenth-century English writer Thomas Carlyle spoke to the modern problem when he opined, "Conviction is worthless unless it is converted into conduct." The number of people who can successfully make decisions independent of their religion or personal philosophy is less than the number of winners in the Publishers Clearing House Sweepstakes.

# Why discriminate against believers?

In the days following the Republican National Convention, a number of voices, liberal and conservative, have been denouncing what they view as an attempt to draft God for the Presidential campaign. Virtually all of them oppose God's candidacy and believe that invoking His name in such a context is a form of political heresy that cannot be tolerated. Some have suggested that past unhealthy marriages of church and state have contributed (at one time or another) to anti-Catholicism, anti-Semitism and Prohibition—to name just a few. They think that a divorce was justified and remarriage is out of the question.

In the words of one writer, ". . . morality should be preached and taught by family and clergy rather than legislated and enforced by politicians and police." Alabama Governor George C. Wallace said much the same thing twenty years ago in arguing against federal desegregation laws.

The question should not be whether morality ought to be imposed; each time a law is passed, somebody's morality is imposed. The question should be: *Whose* morality are we going to impose? Even more to the point, we should ask: What is morality in the first place? Where does it come from?

In some cultures it is considered moral (or at least expedient) to eat, rather than love, one's neighbor. In another culture, it is moral to have more than one wife. In still other cultures it is considered moral to sacrifice humans to gods made of stone. But our forefathers concluded that in order to promote the general welfare some moral code would have to be imposed.

Most Americans are pleased with the progress of civil rights for minorities and the change in attitudes among some people who used to practice their bigotry. But in this debate over the role of God in politics, should we eradicate one form of discrimination and replace it with another? Should we replace "For Whites Only" signs on public restrooms with "For Secularists Only" signs on public institutions? Was not the passage of civil-rights laws one of the greatest impositions of morality in history? Weren't they based on Thomas Jefferson's dictum that "all men are created equal?"

Granted, it may appear unseemly when Sen. Paul Laxalt (R-Nev.) writes a "Dear Christian Leader" letter to clergymen in which he suggests that the Christian thing to do is vote for the reelection of President

117 □ LIBERALS FOR LUNCH

Reagan and Vice President George Bush. But, to be fair, should there not also be criticism of the Rev. Jesse Jackson, whose altar calls have been not for the salvation of souls but for the salvation of the Democratic Party, and whose church offerings have gone for Jackson's political "ministry" and not for the "Lord's work"?

What is the reason for the strong response by conservative religious people to what they perceive as a threat to their own civil rights? A false interpretation, in their view, of the supposed doctrine of church-state separation. They believe that this doctrine has relegated them to a form of second-class citizenship. They view with alarm what they believe have been unconstitutional incursions by the state into territory that was previously reserved for their own moral and religious influence.

What we need is a national debate on subjects that have a moral dimension: abortion, homosexuality, nuclear weapons, and the proper role of religion in politics. Religious people can add a necessary dimension to such a debate. To argue that there have been excesses in the past that can be traced to religious zealotry is no argument at all. No group, no movement, is faultless. Because Prohibition failed is no justification for silencing religious people on such subjects as abortion.

There is a big difference between an individual's right to a drink and the right to take a life. There is a big difference between the religious bigotry of the 1920s and contemporary efforts by conservative believers to exercise the same political rights as atheists. Does anyone believe that Madalyn Murray O'Hair brushes her atheism aside before taking positions on public policy matters? Religious people should be accountable for their misdeeds, but mistakes alone are no reason to throw the religious out with the baptismal water.

Various polls have shown that most journalists have separated themselves from church and synagogue and have no religious world view of their own. That is their individual right. But they should not use their personal antipathy toward God to silence others for whom God is more than a human invention. There is room for both views in a pluralistic culture. Previous and current attempts by conservative Christians and Jews to silence the "ungodly" are as wrong as the desire to banish the "godly" to the outer darkness of nonparticipation in politics.

We should not shy away from this debate; we should welcome it. It is one of our privileges in a free society.

# Will death someday be up to authorities?

You say you can't relate to the controversy surrounding abortion or the killing of the newborn handicapped to satisfy an arbitrary "quality of life" standard?

Can you relate to a system whose philosophy is that old age itself may someday be declared a "handicap"? Let's face it. Unless we are hit by a truck or develop a terminal disease, most of us have a pretty good chance of becoming old. The question is, will there be a widely enough held ethic at that time to ensure that we elderly are treated as something besides garbage that has begun to stink because it has been left around too long?

Not if we continue in the direction in which we have been going.

The number of Americans sixty-five and older has doubled since 1954. The elderly will account for one-fifth of the U.S. population by the year 2030, according to the Census Bureau. With so much pressure on economic resources, including Social Security and Medicare, and far fewer workers to pay the bill, will it not be a simple enough matter for those in power to begin determining who should live and who should die? That's what former New York Senator Jacob Javits wants

to see. That is what Colorado Governor Richard Lamm would like to happen. And that is what a retired (thankfully), but still consulting (unfortunately) surgeon from Cleveland believes should occur.

Dr. George Crile Jr., former head of the Department of General Surgery in Cleveland, told *USA Today* that the older years are unproductive and that unless technological progress ceases, it will be necessary to ration health care.

Then, in what sounds like a page from *Brave New World,* Dr. Crile says, "Cost-effectiveness, when applied to the needs of a society, cannot be based on the effectiveness of the treatment for the individual, but on its effectiveness for the population as a whole."

In other words, if you are forty and need a joint replacement, that will be OK, but if you are seventy and need the same joint, forget it. We'll trade you in on a new model. Imagine the commercial possibilities!

Dr. Crile offers his life philosophy, which might be called a *Consumer Reports* approach to human life: "To view the problem of health rationing objectively, what we need is a concept of man as a colonial creature, similar to ants and bees—which, like ourselves, are so highly specialized and so dependent on one another that no one of them can long survive alone. In the hives and homes of these bees and ants, no special care is given to the aged or infirm. Consideration is for the welfare of the colony as a whole." I'm glad I never got sick in Cleveland when Dr. Crile was practicing.

Der Führer vas right! Let's get on with building the master race where there are no burdens for anybody. Technology has already given us disposable bottles and cans. It is only a matter of conditioning to get us to accept disposable people. No littering, please. Let's help keep America beautiful. We're already well along in this philosophical regression with children. Why leave out Grandmother and Grandfather?

Somewhere between euthanasia and open-ended spending to keep the hearts of the terminally ill pumping away by machine is a middle ground that will protect the dignity and sanctity of human life until its closing moments. But those decisions are best made in an environment where human life is unique and of a value that is different from bees and ants.

I'll give you an illustration. If you were injured in an accident, would you feel more comfortable and reassured if a funeral home ambulance picked you up or an ambulance operated by the local hospital? If you are old and would still enjoy living another year or two (all other things being equal), would you rather have someone looking you over who has the philosophy of life of a Dr. Crile, or would you feel better about the future in the hands of someone whose grandmother is planning to visit her doctor grandson for Thanksgiving?

The time to make these choices is before the future arrives—and it is creeping up on us very fast.

# Exploring young suicides

From Clear Lake, Texas, to New York City, news reports have told of teenagers, many of whom are still too young to vote or drive a car, committing suicide because life has become too great a burden for them to bear.

In three affluent New York counties, eleven young people between the ages of thirteen and twenty have taken their lives since February 4. The New York City Board of Education is planning a "suicide-prevention" program in five high schools and seven junior high schools. It will teach guidance counselors to identify signs of potential victims.

There is a Suicide Research Unit in Rockville, Maryland. It is part of the National Institute of Mental Health. Spokeswoman Dorothy Lewis says there were nearly 6,000 teen suicides in the United States last year. Fifteen percent involved alcohol or drugs. She says that for every "successful" suicide, three times as many teens attempt the act but fail. Women are four to eight times more likely to attempt suicide than men.

The sociological explanations are what you would expect. Teens attempt suicide because of broken homes, humiliation in front of peers by parents, depression, unwanted pregnancies, and problems related to running away from home.

In the New York City Board of Education program and in every other proposal I have read about, all of the efforts to prevent suicide focus on identifying symptoms rather than pinpointing and solving the underlying disease. This is an all-too-common approach in contemporary life. Afraid of getting pregnant? We can't tell you to stop doing what causes pregnancy. That would be "judgmental." Potential suicide? Will we tell the parents to change their lifestyle to benefit their kid and, if we did, would the parents listen?

Dr. James Dobson spent fifteen years at the University of Southern California School of Medicine as a clinical psychologist. He was also associate clinical professor of pediatrics at USC. He leads seminars on the family for the White House staff and has been tapped by the Pentagon as an adviser on military family life.

Dr. Dobson believes the increase in suicide rates among teens is proof of our having become prisoners of the materialistic society in which we live. This materialism, he says, is not rooted in the pursuit of things alone, but it has resulted in the loss of an independent

"WELL, THE STUDY'S WRONG...JUST TELL ME ONE WAY THOSE ARCADES HAVE STIMULATED YOUR CREATIVITY OR IMAGINATION!"

value of human worth. Loss of value, Dr. Dobson believes, has in turn led to a search for worth in beauty, intelligence, success, the "right" clothes, the "right" friends, etc.

Dr. Dobson says lack of self-esteem has undermined the confidence of teens who feel they cannot compete on a materialistic level. Many choose to end their lives rather than suffer the humiliation that comes from seeing themselves as ugly, stupid, poorly dressed, and without the "right" friends.

Adding to their problems, he says, is a lack of spiritual roots in the teen's subculture. Young people want to know who put them here, why they are here, and where they are going. In movies, on television, and in their music they do not find the answers they seek; only more of the materialism that brought on the identity crisis in the first place.

Dr. Dobson says parents and teachers can help prevent most teen suicides if they will make the commitment. He recommends that adults intervene when they see a child's self-esteem shattered, teaching the abusive child to respect every human being regardless of their circumstances. Dr. Dobson says he has personally witnessed adults stand aside and smile while one child verbally abuses another.

One of the recent New York suicide cases is typical. A thirteen-year-old boy was found hanged in the attic of his home. The police said he had written several notes, telling of his despondency over family problems.

In our rush to reach the top, perhaps we should recall the plaintive cry of a child in a popular song of a few years ago: "Daddy, don't you walk so fast . . . daddy, slow down some, 'cause you're making me run, daddy, don't you walk so fast." That goes for Mom?

# Off-key liberal themes

"The fact is that liberalism is at the cross-roads. It will either evolve to meet the issues of the 1980s or it will be reduced to an interesting topic for Ph.D. writing historians."

So said Sen. Paul Tsongas (D-Mass.) before the National Convention of the Americans for Democratic Action on June 14, 1980, less than five months before his prophecy began to unfold at the polls.

If liberals, and particularly those in the Democratic Party, were at the crossroads in 1980, they have traveled a long way down the wrong road in the ensuing four years. They now must come back to the crossroads and take the right road or risk getting lost for a good long time.

Just as conservative Republicans must begin to broaden the base of issues they address to include a genuine concern for the poor and justice for all, so, too, must liberal Democrats begin to shore up their deteriorating base, particularly when it comes to what United Nations Ambassador Jeane Kirkpatrick termed their tendency to "blame America first."

Liberals are perceived as disliking any policy that helps people to make money or to become successful. They apparently believe that prosperity will turn the formerly poor into Republican conservatives, thus diminishing the liberal constituency.

George Gilder addresses this distorted liberal view of reality in his book *Wealth and Poverty*, which budget director David Stockman used to hand out like religious tracts to anyone who would read it.

Mr. Gilder created the Orwellian-sounding phrase, "wealth causes poverty," to demonstrate the warped concept liberals have of the free enterprise system. It is a concept, he says, "for all who seek some alternative to hard work, inequality, thrift, and free exchange as a way of escaping want. How much easier it is—rather than learning the hard lessons of the world—merely to rage at the rich and even to steal from them. How much simpler than diligence and study are the formulas of expropriation! Property is theft. Hate is community. Violence is freedom. Reality is oppression."

This is precisely how most Americans are perceiving the liberal attitude to be. Perhaps that is why they have gone through a metamorphosis and shed their old liberal skin in favor of a new one called "progressive."

Instead of searching for more tax dollars to fund poverty programs which have done little to cure poverty, liberals will need to join with conservatives in forging a healthier economy so that more people can find jobs and enjoy the opportunity to become, if not rich, then at least self-sufficient.

They also will need to be inoculated with some of that Olympic "cheerleading" spirit that overcame much of the gloom and doom of the past that brought us malaise, impotence, and spiritual depression. When was the last time you recall a liberal praising an effort by his own country to sustain or gain freedom for citizens of another country?

The liberal theme has not been "America the Beautiful." Rather, it has echoed a rock song of a few years ago, "You're no good, you're no good, you're no good."

My colleague Patrick J. Buchanan had it right when he said, "To many Americans, the national Democrats seen on network TV are almost un-American and unpatriotic; they appear to relish savaging their own country for real or imagined moral deficiencies. For some reason, the modern liberal feels an obligation to be first, harshest, and least-forgiving in condemning his own country."

As Mr. Buchanan also noted, "The party's problem is not the salesman it has sent out, but the product line it is trying to peddle."

In his book *The Road from Here,* Mr. Tsongas says, ". . . today liberalism is viewed as neither functional nor workable, indeed as a liability . . . That sense of irrelevance affects even successful liberal politicians . . . This is a different generation. And if we do not speak to this generation on its terms, liberalism will decline. And if we do not meet these needs, liberalism should decline."

# Mental junk food in school

Judy Blume writes what she calls "honest" books for children. Others call them something just short of kiddie porn. The Peoria, Illinois, public school system has decided to remove her books from the shelves of its school libraries, saying they are inappropriate for children below the seventh grade because of their sexual content and strong language.

Predictably, the anticensorship thought-police were ready with their statements to the press. After all, what right do parents have to interfere with the state as it attempts to mold the minds of the young and equip them to function properly?

Judith Kruge, director of the American Library Association's Office of Intellectual Freedom, said the association's juvenile division recommends Blume's books for readers as young as nine because of what it says are "her realistic portrayals of young people's problems."

Ask yourself, if you are the parent of a nine-year-old public school student, whether you want your child reading this from *Deenie,* one of Blume's books: "I turned away from the kitchen door and ran back to my room. As soon as I got into bed I started touching my-self. I have this special place and when I rub it I get a very nice feeling. I don't know what it's called or if anyone else has it but when I have trouble falling asleep, touching my special place helps a lot."

Kids have also been known to fall asleep while having their backs rubbed by a parent, but rubbing one's genitalia sells more books and apparently is the only reality Blume knows. Later in the book, the kids openly discuss masturbation in a classroom setting. The teacher encourages them to be frank. They are.

Why must "reality" always be one-dimensional? Why must books awaken sexual interest before some children's curiosity is aroused? Once awakened, why is it that chastity until marriage and caring enough for another person not to engage in premarital sex are not considered reality? Why do the "educators" assume that kids are just itching to jump into bed with one another? Why are these "problems" solved by urging children to respond only to their glands?

The mother of a ten-year-old girl in Rohnert Park, California, complained that she had not been informed of the availability of Blume's books in her daughter's elementary school. The principal told the woman that

his secretary had examined the books, looking for references to God. Finding none, the book was approved. Do some kids consider God a reality in their lives? Do principals consider God to be more hazardous to one's health than the consequences of sexual experimentation?

Authors do not write in a vacuum. They have values, beliefs, and lifestyles they want the reader to accept. Judy Blume has been divorced twice. She is currently having what she euphemistically calls a "relationship" with a man to whom she is not married. In a recent interview, Blume said that when she wrote her first adult novel, *Wifey,* she had stopped believing in the possibility of monogamous, long-term relationships.

As to the possibility of getting married for the third time, Blume says that it "makes me shudder. It's against everything I believe in." Are such values transmitted through Blume's books for children? Many parents think so.'

Critics label as "lunatic" the Peoria decision to remove the Blume books from the school libararies. They say the books are available at public libraries and in bookstores. That is not the point. The point is whether children who are required by law to go to schools paid for by the taxpayers should be taught values at such a young age that conflict with what many parents teach and believe; values, it could be debated, that are against the best interests of the child.

Arguing that Blume is just giving the kids what they want is no argument at all. Many schools have banned junk-food vending machines as unhealthful to children's bodies. If parents want their children to read Judy Blume, let them buy her books or take their kids to the public library. In public schools, the children will learn far more from studying the classics than from the mental junk food dished out by Judy Blume.

# The (in)credibility of news

Television anchorpersons from the three networks recently got together in New York for a discussion on the credibility of their industry. In recent years, journalists have vied with used car dealers and loan sharks for last place in the credibility poll.

The network news stars acknowledged that "there has been an abuse of privilege, and we are addressing an increasingly hostile environment in which there is not much appreciation at this moment for the role of the press in this country" (NBC's Tom Brokaw), and "There is a tendency to focus on the horse race (ratings) rather than the quality of the news" (ABC's Peter Jennings), and "The real question is: How far can we go without tarnishing our journalistic integrity?" (CBS's Bill Kurtis). Not to worry, Bill. The damage has already been done.

In a cover story a year ago, *Time* magazine correctly stated the problem faced by journalism when it headlined, "A growing perception of arrogance threatens the American press." *Time* quoted a woman who had written to a major newspaper: "Journalists are so out of touch with majority values, such as honor, duty and service to country, that they are alienated from the very society that they purport to serve."

Tom Brokaw seemed to prove the woman correct when he told the radical left-wing *Mother Jones* magazine in April 1983 that President Reagan's values are "simplistic and old-fashioned." Wonder how he felt on election night when so many of those dumb folks voted for Reagan?

Many people see contemporary journalists infected with what U.N. Ambassador Jeane Kirkpatrick called the "blame America first" syndrome. They see highly paid reporters frequently trashing the country that allows them to earn huge amounts of money while touting the supposed virtues of nations under Communist domination or embroiled in revolution.

It is not that America is above criticism. What causes so many to grit their teeth is the perception that reporters seem incapable of discovering anything good about their own land. This is why press credibility suffers.

The English poet Samuel Taylor Coleridge said one must exercise a "willing suspension of disbelief" in reading his work because of its often fantasylike quality.

Many of today's journalists seem to be asking their viewers/readers to exercise a willing suspension of *belief* and not to believe in anything unless the reporters tell them it is so.

During the Nixon Administration, I recall Treasury Secretary John Connally admonishing a group of reporters that they had a responsibility to be "cheerleaders" for the free enterprise system. No, they don't. But neither do they have a responsibility to be denigrators of it.

Wes Pippert, of United Press International, has said that there is a difference between cynicism and skepticism. Unfortunately for the press and the public it is supposed to serve, that distinction has been lost, and cynicism seems to dominate contemporary journalism.

The reason why the press is perceived as arrogant is because many times it is. The reason why so many ethics courses are now springing up in college journalism curriculums (from sixty-nine to 114 in the past seven years) is because of the eroding credibility of the press.

Reporters do not have to be cheerleaders or boosters of a President or party. But a good reporter will do his or her best to be fair, even though the reporter, like all of us, finds it impossible to be objective.

All too often, though, when the press is attacked, instead of dealing with the reason for the criticism, journalists prefer to hide behind the First Amendment, pretending they are answerable to no one. Such an attitude gives immediate license to any adolescent who wants to join a small paper or radio station, apply for a press card, and assume the position of an untouchable. It is this attitude and this frivolous approach to freedom of the press that has put journalism in hot water.

A little humility and acknowledgment of occasional wrongdoing coupled with attempts to correct it would ease the pressure journalism feels. A strong and credible press must be preserved because it is an underlying source of strength to a free society. But as the late Bishop Fulton Sheen said, "No freedom is ever given without an accompanying responsibility."

# 'Tis the season

Time was when you could sense the advent of Christmas by the department store decorations which went up the day after Halloween, or when signs began to appear announcing that only 100 shopping days remained.

As with so many other things, times have changed. Today, one senses that Christmas is coming by observing how the American Civil Liberties Union and other guardians of "free speech" are preparing to limit how some people can celebrate it. 'Tis the season to be litigious.

The Supreme Court has agreed to decide whether a small, wealthy, and heavily Jewish suburb of Scarsdale, New York, should be required to allow a Nativity scene in the center of town. The case is the reverse of one in Pawtucket, Rhode Island, where government officials wanted the display but the litigants did not, and the Supreme Court said it was O.K. because the Nativity was part of a wider celebration that included secular elements.

In suburban Scarsdale, officials don't want it, even though they have accommodated it for twenty-four years. The Nativity has been located on public property, but paid for with private funds from local Protestant and Roman Catholic churches.

The 2nd U.S. Circuit Court of Appeals said last June that Scarsdale must allow the display because the park is a public forum and its use cannot be denied to any group solely because of the content of the group's speech. The town has appealed to the Supreme Court, saying that "the fact that a Nazi has the right to speak in a public forum would entail mechanically the right to plant a six-foot square swastika in the park for a week or so around the anniversary of Hitler's birthday." But the content of one group's speech should not be limited by citing the outrageous content of another group's speech.

A recent decision by the San Francisco Board of Supervisors might bring these cases into better focus. The supervisors recently voted 10-1 to prohibit a Nativity scene from being erected at City Hall, but the city will continue to allow the display of a menorah on public property for the annual observance of Hannukah.

Think for a moment about the media and public outcry had it been the Jewish religious symbol that was prohibited in San Francisco and the Christian one

"I'M AFRAID IF WE SLAP A LAW SUIT ON THIS ONE WE'LL GET THE WHOLE
COUNTRY RILED UP... THEY'RE USING A CABBAGE PATCH KID FOR JESUS!"

allowed. Cries of anti-Semitism would have stretched from coast to coast.

Because it is a Christian religious symbol that is banned in San Francisco (and attempts to ban it are being made in Scarsdale, New York), we hear no alarm sounded by the civil liberties equivalent of airport metal detectors through which all speech must pass. Surely if it is anti-Semitism to ban a symbol of Judaism from public property, is it not fair to label the banning of a Christian religious symbol anti-Christian bigotry?

In the Pawtucket case, Chief Justice Burger said that the supposed "wall" separating church and state is not absolute and that the state has an obligation to "accommodate" religion. So long as public property is available to all religions, there can be no harm done to religion or to the Constitution by allowing its free exercise.

But when activist groups and the courts cooperate to deny Christians the right to display Nativity scenes or sing Christmas carols in school (along with Hannukah songs, of course), then that is unfair, unwise, and unconstitutional.

As Constitutional attorney William Ball has said, a basic fact has been ignored in these cases, and that is the denial of the religious aspirations of the American people. Says Ball, "This means that we are to be only a secularly disciplined society."

Recent Supreme Court decisions involving tuition tax credits, paid chaplains in state legislatures, and Nativity scenes on public property indicate that the court may be interested in reversing the trend toward forced secularism, a trend it apparently believes has gone too far. The fact that it has chosen to accept so many church-state cases this term may be an indication that it wishes to atone for previous misdeeds.

# Cal Thomas and Wayne Stayskal

CAL THOMAS is a veteran of 21 years in the field of broadcast journalism. His excellent work as an investigative reporter and anchorman for NBC and its affiliates has been recognized by the Associated Press, United Press International, and Headliners, among other organizations. Thomas is currently the Vice President for Communications at Moral Majority, Inc., and also writes a column for the Los Angeles Times Syndicate twice a week. Other books by Cal Thomas include: **A Freedom Dream** (Word), **Public Persons and Private Lives** (Word), and **Book Burning** (Crossway Books). He and his wife Ray live with their four children in Virginia.

WAYNE STAYSKAL is an editorial cartoonist with the Tampa Tribune. His cartoons have been syndicated nationally since 1962, and several collections of his work have been published: **Trim's Arena, Hey, How Come They Get Steak and We Get Chicken?**, and **It Said Another Bad Word.** Max McCrohon, editor and Chicago Tribune executive, once called Stayskal "the epitome of all that is best in modern newspaper cartooning ... A reader feels Stayskal has a basic faith in his fellowman." The cartoons inside **Liberals for Lunch** are selected from the best of Stayskal's pointedly humorous work.